Night Fire Morning Snow
The Road to Chosin

Mark Scott Smith

Rolling Wave Books

ISBN 978-0-578-37035-4

All maps are from Wikimedia Commons or Google.
Back cover: Wikimedia image from Chinese Military Science Academy.

This work of historical fiction is dedicated to my wife Holly for her invaluable support, research assistance and excellent suggestions regarding the manuscript.

The cold earth slept below;
above the cold sky shone;
And all around,
With a chilling sound,
From caves of ice and fields of snow
The breath of night like death did flow
Beneath the sinking moon.

Percy Bysshe Shelley

TIMELINE OF KOREAN WAR

June 1950 - North Korean forces cross the 38th Parallel and invade South Korea

September 1950 - US/UN/ROK forces pushed back to the southern tip of the Korean peninsula at Busan

September 1950 - General MacArthur launches the Inchon invasion and forces North Korean forces to flee north

October 1950 - MacArthur orders his troops into Korea's northernmost provinces near the border with China

November 1950 - US Marine and Army forces surrounded by Chinese Communist troops at the Chosin (Changjin) Reservoir

January-June 1951 - See-saw battles back and forth with Seoul changing hands four times

April 1951 - General MacArthur relieved of UN command

July 1951 - Truce talks begin, but fighting along the 38th parallel continues for two more years

July 1953 - Armistice signed at Panmunjom

Britannica.com

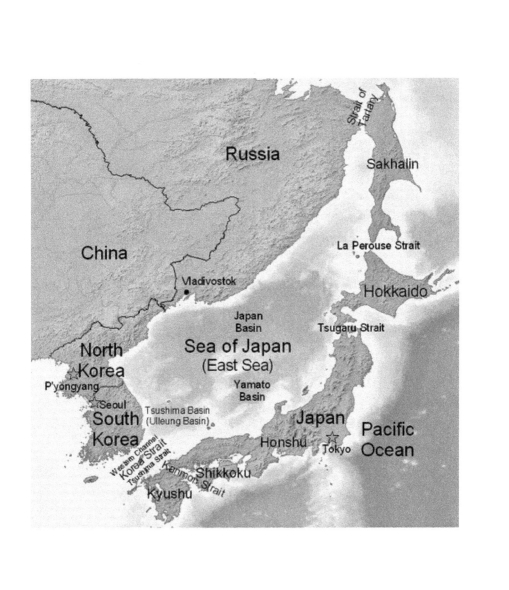

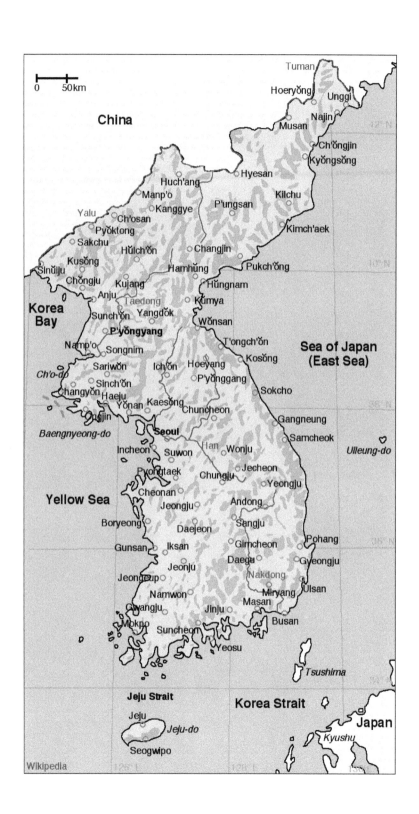

1940

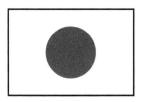

Chapter One
Heijō

KALGAN CHINA—*After capturing the city of Wu Yuan, Japanese forces dealt repeated blows to the enemy, who have lost much of their fighting spirit and are now wandering about in desert plains.*

Japan Times
March 17, 1940

Pyongyang, Chōsen (Japanese occupied Korea)
March 24, 1940

Ho-jun stepped down from the streetcar in his hometown Pyongyang (renamed *Heijō* by the Japanese colonizers) and strolled along the familiar sidewalks of his youth. It had been a while since he'd last been home. Medical school in Seoul (named *Keijō* by the Japanese) was an all-consuming affair.

How good it felt to be strolling these streets once again under an overcast sky and a comfortable temperature of 9 degrees C. He unbuttoned his woolen greatcoat and blended into the light crowd out for a Sunday stroll. A bearded man in baggy trousers, a flowing, white overcoat and tall horsehair hat, strode by like a great white heron. One step behind, his wife, hatless, in a high-waisted white dress pushed a small wooden cart. Most pedestrians however, wore Western-style clothes—casual shirts and trousers for the men; dresses just below the knee for women and exaggerated shoulder pads for both sexes.

Ho-jun glanced cross the street at two Japanese soldiers in tan uniforms, high leather boots and white armbands that identified them as the dreaded *Kempeitai* (a force composed of both military and secret police). The soldiers stood aside watching a dozen children carry small, wooden crosses into the sanctuary of a Presbyterian Church. *Christ the Lord is risen today. Alleluia!* The children sang in exuberant Korean. Ho-jun had almost forgotten. It was Easter Sunday.

At midday, the *White Crane* restaurant was moderately crowded, but fortunately, a table was free in Ho-jun's favorite corner. Removing his coat and shoes, he walked across the wooden floor behind a smiling waitress wearing a vibrant blue *hanbok*, the traditional Korean dress with long sashes laced just above her breasts. Seated on a cushion in front of a low table, he ordered a bottle of *soju*, a colorless beverage distilled from fermented rice that was greater than 40% alcohol by volume. When the bottle arrived, he held a wooden cup with both hands as the waitress bowed, then poured. Turning his head to one side, he covered his mouth and quaffed the entire cup. With a polite bow of his head, he thanked the waitress and settled back to wait for his childhood friend Lee Kwang-min to arrive.

When Ho-jun saw Kwang-min come through the door of the White Crane in his Imperial Japanese Army uniform, he momentarily turned away to hide a look of unexpected shock.

Kwang-min's once-handsome face now had a jagged scar, elevated like the Taebaek Mountain range, arcing across the left side of his face from his upper lip halfway across his cheek.

Ho-jun sprang to his feet and bowed, then grasped his friend's forearm and shook his hand vigorously. "Kwang-min! I was so sorry to hear you were wounded. How are you doing now, my dear friend?"

Kwang-min smiled. "Much better now, thanks. I'll be finishing my rehabilitation here soon."

Ho-jun examined the scar on Kwang-min's face. "What happened to you?"

"Chinese Bayonet." Kwang-min pointed to his leg. "He also got me here before I shot him. Most of my rehabilitation has been about the leg." He straightened up. "But now I'm back almost 100%. Soon I'll be returned to active duty—probably to fight bandits in Manchukuo."

The two long-time friends spent the next few hours catching up, reminiscing about their school days in Pyongyang, their near win in the Korean High School Basketball finals and news of their families and friends. After countless cigarettes and three bottles of soju, the conversation turned toward the stale-mated war between Imperial Japan and the Chinese.

"What's it like?" Ho-jun hesitated. "Having to kill men."

Kwang-min spoke in a measured tone. "It's kill, or be killed, Ho-jun. I killed a lot of men. I'm not proud of it, but I did my duty."

Ho-jun grasped his friend's wrist. His words were intense but slightly garbled by the soju "You're doing your duty for the Imperial Japanese Army. *Not* Korea. Don't forget that."

Kwang-min swept his friend's arm away. "What about you then? Attending a Japanese university and going on to Tokyo for more training?"

"Keijo University is the best medical school in Korea," Ho-jun muttered. "And how can I turn down infectious disease training in Tokyo?"

Kwang-min nodded brusquely. "Exactly. And how can *I* turn down an equally excellent opportunity? The Imperial Japanese Army is the best in Asia."

At 1800, as the sun began to set, the two friends parted. Despite a few flare-ups as they stirred the embers, they had rekindled the fire of their long-time friendship. Who knew when they would meet again?

Before returning to his parents' hillside home, Ho-jun decided to walk through nearby Moran Park and clear his head. Although it was acceptable for young men to drink heavily on social occasions, his father, a practitioner of traditional Korean medicine, would no doubt lecture him should he come home obviously intoxicated.

Above the steep granite steps at the entrance to the park, he soon found himself on a trail, winding upward through the woods toward a familiar childhood lookout surrounded by cherry trees that were just beginning to blossom. Ho-jun gazed down at the lights of the city. Soon his thoughts returned to his childhood friend. Had it really been four years since they'd seen each other? Kwang-min had always wanted to be a soldier. And now, despite great danger, he seemed to be doing it well.

Ho-jun had to admit his criticism of his friend's service in the Japanese Army was hypocritical. Both felt they were pursuing honorable careers within the Imperial Japanese system. Nevertheless, though each considered himself a Korean nationalist, neither of them was making a statement against the oppression of Japanese colonialism. With a sigh, he headed back down the trail.

At the foot of the stone staircase leading up to his parents tiled-roof *Hanok*-style house, Ho-jun stretched his shoulders and straightened his back. He had to smile. How many times had he raced Kwang-min up these steps?

The housemaid Nari opened the heavy wooden gate on Ho-jun's second knock. With a bow, she ushered him through the inner courtyard, past flowering plum trees and potted forsythia shrubs, to the stone stairway leading up to the main house. Nari opened the door of his father's examination room, ushered Ho-jun into the small anteroom and disappeared with a final bow.

"Ah, Ho-jun," his father said. "Just in time to offer a diagnosis."

A young woman in a stylish yellow hanbok bowed as she held a baby in her arms. "Is this another doctor?" She asked.

Ho-jun's father smiled. "You are in luck, *manim*. This is my son, a doctor in Western medicine. You may now have two opinions." He turned to Ho-jun. "This baby has fevers, nasal discharge and irritability. My pulse diagnosis suggests an imbalance in the flow of *Ki* through the respiratory tract. See what you think."

7

Ho-jun examined the child. Active and alert, aside from an obvious common cold, he had no abnormal findings. "I agree father. He has an upper respiratory infection."

His father smiled and turned toward the mother. "I will give your baby some medicine to restore a healthy balance of energy." He selected a packet of herbs from his cabinet. "Give him half a spoonful of this powder in a cup of warm water every eight hours. It's called echinacea."

The woman took the packet, paid a few *yen* and bowed her way out of the room.

"I'm glad we agree on a diagnosis for once," his father said. "Let's go to the main hall. Your mother and sister are there."

Although he had doubts about the efficacy of echinacea, Ho-jun said nothing. It wouldn't hurt anything and there was no effective alternate therapy for the common cold in Western medicine. Besides, it felt good to get along pleasantly with his father.

His mother and adolescent sister Jung-soon were in the narrow, main hall, sitting on a low-lying sofa of finely carved elm. Close to the heated floor, they were surrounded by silk-covered cushions and bathed in the soft glow of the city, filtering through the leaded glass windows like a river of blue light.

With a smile, Ho-jun strode across the room and bowed deeply before his mother. "Good evening, *Umma*." His bow was less deep toward his sister. "How are you, *yeodongsaeng*?" He asked, using the informal speech of siblings.

Ho-jun settled into the sofa, took tea and joined the discussion which was focused on Jung-soon's attire. "It's entirely too western," their mother said. "Even the Japanese are reverting to traditional dress these days." She turned toward Ho-jun. "What do you think, Ho-jun?"

Ho-jun leaned back, regarding Jung-soon's hair, her dress, her shoes. He loved his little sister. "I think she looks like a modern high school girl, Umma."

"Oh, Ho-jun. You always take her side," their mother said with a gentle laugh.

His father joined the group. "Tell us more about the training in Japan."

Ho-jun described the infectious disease training he was about receive in Tokyo thanks to his mentor Professor Furukawa. Unlike other instructors in the Imperial Japanese Medical School, the professor encouraged ethnic Korean students to excel academically. Ho-jun ranked at the top of his class.

"I'd like to go to college in Tokyo," Jung-soon said.

"We'll see," her mother said.

Ho-jun was content. His family seemed to be doing well. With the recent revival of interest in herbs due to wartime shortages of standard medications, his father's medical practice was thriving. His mother seemed content running the household, parenting an emancipating, teenage daughter and digging in her garden. And his sister was developing into a charming, young woman. Despite some minor conflicts, his was a harmonious family.

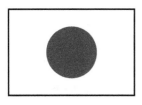

Chapter Two
Keijo

TOKYO—*War Minister Hata stated: "In governing our overseas possessions we are following the principle of treating the colonial peoples the same as the people at home with a view to placing them on intimate terms. Both in Korea and Formosa the government is constantly endeavoring to have them become true imperial subjects and as a matter of fact, satisfactory progress is being made in this connection."*
                          Japan Times
                          March 6, 1940

Keijō Imperial University School of Medicine
Keijō (Seoul) Korea
March 25, 1940

Senior medical student Choi Ho-Jun folded his stethoscope into the pocket of his long white coat and clomped down the steep staircase to the pathology laboratory in the basement of the University Hospital. He didn't want to be late for medical rounds with Professor Furukawa during his last week of training at the Keijō Imperial University.

With a bow toward his teacher, Ho-jun joined his four medical student teammates who were all of Japanese origin. The team gathered around a ceramic pot that sat on a black slate countertop. The pungent, odor of formaldehyde burned Ho-jun's nostrils as he and the other students leaned over the pot to view its contents—a kidney, spleen and heart.

The medical students draped themselves with surgical aprons and pulled on rubber gloves as Professor Furukawa began the session. "This is an opportunity to formulate a diagnosis based on pathology you can identify with careful examination of the anatomical specimens. Take your time, gentlemen. And try to think systematically."

Ho-jun carefully slid both gloved hands into the pot to cradle a torn kidney that had been bi-valved by the pathologist's scalpel. Laying the kidney on a white towel, he trailed his fingertips over two deep-red, wedge-shaped lesions that spread their wings against the outer margins of the specimen like dark butterflies. "Looks like we have infarcts in the renal cortex," he said.

"Let's take a look at the heart," a student said.

"And the spleen," another suggested.

It didn't take the students long to identify the infarcts in the mesentery and spleen. With an enlarged left atrium and growth on the stenotic mitral valve, the obvious diagnosis was endocarditis—an infection of heart tissue that was already ravaged by rheumatic fever. Endemic to Korea, rheumatic fever was a disease the students knew quite well. Gross infarcts in the kidneys and spleen were common when damaged valves became infected.

Ho-jun bowed to Professor Furukawa. "We have a diagnosis, Professor—bacterial endocarditis in a heart damaged by rheumatic fever."

Although his face reflected little emotion, Professor Furukawa's eyes seemed to lighten with approval. "Excellent, gentlemen. While easy to see on a postmortem specimen, this diagnosis is often elusive in clinical practice. The symptoms and signs are not always typical. And many are similar to those found in other diseases. But, as in this case, a predisposing valve disorder is observed in the majority of bacterial endocarditis cases." He looked intently at the medical students gathered around the table. "Shall we go up on the ward now and examine a living patient with this disease?"

On the medical unit, three floors above, the team stood behind their professor as he attempted to elicit a medical history from a pale, middle-aged Korean man with cheeks the color of a radish in springtime. When it became obvious the man did not understand Japanese well, the professor asked Ho-jun to translate. It began with a low-grade fever six months earlier, the man said; then fatigue, back pain, and weight loss.

Ho-jun waited as each member of the team evaluated the patient, then, proceeding with a polite bow, he performed his own brief physical examination. Except for a few dark-red lines crossing the nail beds, he found nothing significantly abnormal on the external exam. However, applying the bell of his stethoscope to the patient's chest, he heard an opening snap of the second heart sound followed by a low-pitched rumble that faded away like the underwater song of a distant whale—the classic murmur of mitral valve stenosis.

Ignoring the patient, Professor Furukawa launched into a Socratic-style discussion of bacterial endocarditis, eliciting teaching points from the students themselves. Of what symptoms would your patient complain? What would you find on physical examination? What laboratory test might you want? What would be your differential diagnosis? What treatment could you offer?

Regarding the last question, a student suggested sulfonamides. "A logical choice," the professor said. "Unfortunately, they've proven ineffective in this disease." The professor turned from the bedside, leading his team off the ward.

Ho-jun smiled and bowed briefly toward the patient as they left his bedside. He felt uneasy. Shouldn't they have offered some reassurance? Would the professor have interacted differently with a Japanese patient?

Dark clouds, their underbellies illuminated by the setting sun, passed over the street in the Myeong-dong district as Ho-jun took Sun-ja's elbow, gently steering her around an elderly woman with a bandaged leg and an old man trudging along beneath a heavy pack loaded with kindling. Scattered groups of people bundled up against the cold walked along the sidewalk, shopping or heading home after work.

Every few blocks, a Japanese Kempeitai military policeman, the red letters on his white armband alerting wary passersby, scanned the crowd. More ominous, the Tokkō, undercover thought police, seemed to be everywhere. City police, Koreans in blue uniforms, were often more helpful than threatening, but everyone feared the Kempeitai and the Tokkō. A Korean, had to be very careful what he said these days.

Just a few blocks from the Meiji Cinema, tattered posters still proclaimed the *1940 Olympics and Grand International Exposition of Japan,* months after both events were canceled because of the ongoing war in China. But the movies were still quite popular. A long line stood in front of the ornately resplendent, six-floor, 1500-seat theater.

Ho-jun grudgingly admired the entrepreneurial energy of the Japanese colonists. Despite harsh and repressive rule, they brought significant progress to Korea including modern industrial, transportation, agricultural and public health techniques, nationwide electricity and universal education. Unfortunately, with Japan mired in a vicious war in eastern China, most of Korea's natural resources, industrial output and agricultural yield was being exported to Japan.

But it was the brutal repression of anything perceived by the military or secret police as "anti-Japanese" that ignited Ho-jun's patriotism. Although none of his close friends or family had been harassed, he knew of several people who were imprisoned, tortured, or even killed for expressing dissident ideas. And now the Japanese were increasing pressure for cultural assimilation. *One body, one spirit*—they exhorted Koreans. A recent ordinance "encouraged" Koreans to change their family names to resemble the Japanese style. Although not compulsory, registration for official identification or ration cards now required a Japanese-style name.

For these reasons, once a month, for the past year, Ho-jun attended secret meetings of the Gwangju Student Independence Movement. Labelled "study groups," the meetings were carefully rotated between clandestine locations. Names and addresses were never recorded. Although some members were communists, most were simply nationalists like him. Activities included sharing information, distributing anti-Japanese pamphlets, or raising funds to support Korean guerrillas fighting Imperial Japanese forces in Manchukuo.

Ho-jun had few opportunities to discuss his true feelings about Japanese colonialism—obviously, he couldn't talk with his childhood friend Kwang-min who was now in the Imperial Japanese Army. And that's why he was looking forward to an evening with Sun-ja, a nursing student he'd befriended in the Korean independence movement. Since ethnic Koreans were in the distinct minority in colonial medical and nursing schools, Ho-jun and Sun-ja had many experiences in common. Although he wasn't in love with Sun-ja, their relationship was intimate and sincere. Tonight he was glad to be taking her to the controversial film entitled *Tuition* that dared to have Korean characters speak their native language rather than Japanese.

After the film, bundled up in woolen hats and coats, Ho-jun and Sun-ja walked to a nearby noodle house. Over steaming bowls of *janchi guksu* soup and sips of soju wine, they discussed the film.

"That village was a lot like where I grew up," Sun-ja said. "It's a hard life for most people there."

Ho-jun shrugged. "I guess my family was fairly well off in Pyongyang. And here I am, a typical, *chungin* medical student. May I pour you some more wine, nurse?"

Sun-ja laughed. "Certainly, Doctor." She leaned over and lowered her silky voice. "Wasn't it wonderful to see our actors speak Korean?"

"Yes! It took courage to make that film."

Sun-ja wrinkled her forehead. "Do you think it just sneaked past the Japanese censors?"

"Maybe. But it might be the message they want to promote. A nice, Japanese teacher goes out of his way to help a destitute Korean boy obtain tuition for school. A warm and uplifting story. No mention of war. Nothing about oppression."

Sun-ja laid a hand on his wrist and subtly shook her head. "We're in a public space," she whispered. "The thought police particularly like restaurants."

Ho-jun lowered his head. "I'm sorry. Was I talking too loud?"

Sun-ja nodded.

March 28, 1940

Ho-jun hurried along Daehak-ro to his last preventive medicine lecture. Halfway across an intersection, a strong gust of wind caught his umbrella, turning it inside out. Pausing to straighten the umbrella back into shape, he glanced ahead at a man standing on the corner. *Dodaeche?* A student he recognized from clandestine meetings of the Independence Movement was beckoning him with a subtle tip of his cap. What was he doing here? It was agreed that members of the movement would avoid public encounters. Kempeitai and

Tokkō agents were everywhere—maybe even in the student body.

The young man looked out over the intersection without making eye contact as Ho-jun strolled by. "They've taken Sun-ja," he murmured.

A thunderbolt shot through Ho-jun's chest and seared his heart. He increased his pace down the street onto the grounds of the university. The clouds were swirling in the sky. Pulse racing, he sat on a bench outside the University Hospital and slowed his breathing, trying to calm down. Then he remembered. The emergency contact! Dangerous, but his only real option. He headed for the Dapsimni-dong district.

With trembling hands, Ho-jun opened the door to a dimly lit antique store that held art, furniture and jewelry from days gone by. The owner, an older Korean man with silver hair, was engaged in conversation with a well-dressed Japanese woman regarding an ornately carved cedar chest. Ho-jun turned toward a display case and feigned interest in a copper brooch studded with tiny emeralds.

"I'll be right with you, sir," the antique dealer said.

When the Japanese customer left, the antique dealer spoke tersely to Ho-jun. "You shouldn't be here unless it's an emergency."

"The police have taken Yun Sun-ja," Ho-jun said. "What can I…"

The antique dealer cut him off with a wave of his hand. "Nothing. You can do nothing. I'll see what I can find out. Wait until you hear from me. Now be gone."

Ho-jun walked aimlessly along the banks of the Han River, his mind awhirl with conflict and anxiety. Halfway across the

Mapo bridge, he leaned against the railing to watch pelicans glide just above the water. Along the southern bank of the river, cherry trees were just beginning to blossom. He felt powerless. How could he help Sun-ja? Walking into the jaws of the secret police would be foolish and futile. And what if she'd given up names under torture? Was he also in danger? Medical school graduation was only two days away. What about his upcoming training in Tokyo?

The next morning a Japanese medical student in Ho-jun's graduating class approached him in the hallway of the University Hospital. "Did you hear the terrible news?" The student said. "One of our nursing students was attacked up in Samcheong Park. She died in a police car on the way to the hospital."

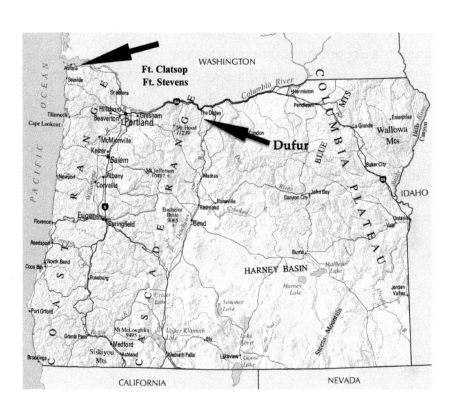

Chapter Three
Always ready. Always there!

WASHINGTON—*General George C. Marshall, Army Chief of Staff, said yesterday it was "essential" that President Roosevelt receive authority to call out the National Guard, if needed, because of "the recognized possibility of dangerous developments in this hemisphere."*

New York Times
June 2, 1940

Fort Clatsop, Oregon
June 8, 1940

Fresh out of high school in the Columbia River Gorge, Private Nick Jackson lay prone on the firing range at the National Guard training center on the northwest coast of Oregon. He looked up at a single cirrus cloud slowly dissipating above the ocean, then focused on the target 200 yards down the dusty rifle range. On the target, three dark lines formed shapes which were layered one within the other. The innermost shape, filled with a solid black color, vaguely resembled a human head and torso. Nick focused on the torso.

This was Nick's last shot in the rifleman's qualification course. He wouldn't know the results until the final tally, but his gut feeling was good. He'd fired his first rifle when he was ten years old. And years of elk hunting with his father had taught him stealth and patience.

Nick anchored the butt of his World War One Springfield rifle in the pocket of his shoulder and aligned his right eye through the rifle's sights. His father's words came as they always had on the hunt. *Keep both eyes open and relax all your muscles.* Nick took two deep breaths in and out. With the last exhalation, he gently squeezed the trigger.

After the drill sergeant's cease fire command, several guardsmen darted out from cover to score the targets. By the time Nick had field stripped, cleaned, lubricated and reassembled his rifle, his drill sergeant was standing before him.

"Not bad, Jackson. You hit 29 of 40 targets. Enjoy your Saturday night leave." The drill sergeant began to stride away, then stopped and pivoted. "Of course, 30 would've got you a sharpshooter badge."

Dismissed from the rifle range, the guardsmen began to head back to camp. Spirits were high. Like Nick, most would be getting ready for a Saturday night on the town. His longtime, childhood friend Jim Anderson had assured him his girlfriend would line him up with a swell date for the movies in Astoria. After two weeks of intense training, it was time to take a break.

"Hey buddy. Ready for a big night?" Jim Anderson clapped Nick on the back as they walked toward the post. "Did you qualify for Marksman?"

Nick gave a casual nod. "Yeah. I passed."

"I got 23 hits out of 40. How about you?"

Nick tilted his head to one side and smiled. "29."

Jim's head snapped back. "Jeez! You're really up there, pal! Maybe you should be a sniper. You know—camouflaged with leaves on your head, up in a tree?"

Nick punched Jim lightly on the arm. "Very funny. You know that's the last thing I want to do."

Jim stopped walking. "What *do* you want to do, buddy?"

Nick shrugged. "Who knows? I'll be at Marylhurst College this fall. A couple of extra bucks a month from the Guard will help make ends meet. And I don't mind two weeks of summertime training. It's a little bit like football. But a military career? Not in the cards for me, pal."

"Guess I feel about the same," Jim said. "But the way things are going in Europe right now, makes me wonder if we're going to have much choice."

Nick hitched the leather strap of his rifle further up his shoulder. "Don't forget about Japan. Looks like they're eyeballing the East Indies now that Holland's gone down to the Germans." He patted his rifle. "And moving our fleet to Pearl Harbor won't do diddly squat about it."

After a hot shower and a change into dapper civvies—high-waisted slacks and open collar shirts—Nick and Jim were cruising north on Highway 101 in Jim's 1935 Ford sedan.

"The girls said they'd meet us in front of the Liberty for the seven o'clock show," Jim said.

Nick fiddled with the radio dial, tuning up and down through bursts of static, plaintive country songs and Christian messages before he settled on Frank Sinatra's *I'll never smile again* on KFJI from Astoria. "So tell me about my date, Jim."

"Well, I haven't really met her, you know. But Angie says she's really nice and quite a looker."

A large billboard along the roadside had Uncle Sam, sleeves rolled up and fists balled tight, proclaiming *Defend Your Country. Enlist Now. US Army.*

"There you go, buddy," Jim said with a wry glance toward the billboard.

Nick's laugh was disdainful. "Hell. We don't need to enlist. General Marshall says we can be called up anytime."

As promised, the girls were waiting in front of the Liberty Theater, an Italian Renaissance-styled building on Commercial Street that once featured vaudeville.

Jim's girl Angie looked great in a summer dress with padded shoulders, a small waist and flared hips. Nick's date Ruth had straight, soft, chestnut brown hair that swirled across her neck as she turned her head from side to side. Beneath her slightly upturned nose, light pink lipstick accentuated the graceful contour of her lips. As she turned on wedge sandals, her-blue linen dress swept softly across the contour of her hips. Nick flashed a quick smile at Jim. Ruth was a real dish.

Angie and Ruth, who had just graduated from high school in Warrenton, had summer jobs in Astoria on the ferry that crossed the Columbia River to Washington.

"She's on the boat," Ruth said. "I just take tickets at the dock."

Remembering his mother's advice, Nick tried to stand tall and handsome. Not only was Ruth good looking; she was smart and very friendly.

On the brightly lit theater marquee, *The Grapes of Wrath* was written in large block letters with the subtitle *John Steinbeck*. A sign above the ticket booth read: price of a ticket $0.24.

"I've got a fin," Jim said, flashing a five-dollar bill at Nick. "How about you covering a bite to eat afterward?"

"No beef here. I can see you've got the big moolah."

Angie nudged Jim. "Ruth and I can chip in."

"Yeah. We don't mind going Dutch," Ruth said.

"Don't worry about it," Jim said, handing the five dollar bill to the cashier.

Inside the theater, the women insisted on buying snacks—popcorn, Cokes, Three Musketeers, Fifth Avenue and a Mounds Bar. Total cost 60 cents.

The newsreel, highlighting the battle for Norway, was a bit outdated and the Donald Duck window washer cartoon was only funny when a bumblebee got stuck inside his workman's hat. But they all thought *The Grapes of Wrath* was excellent.

The sun was an orange glow flattening against the northern horizon when they came out of the theater around 9 PM. A light breeze off the Columbia River swept over Nick's face as he took Ruth's arm to cross the street. A warm sensation spread throughout his body. He loved being with Ruth. So smart. So beautiful. So nice.

"What say we hit Thiel's for a bite?" Jim said.

"Sounds good to me," Nick said.

"Okay," Angie said. "But this time we're definitely going Dutch."

"No dice," Nick said. "It's my turn."

Thiel's Restaurant was fairly empty as they settled into a booth. Nick and Ruth sipped cokes and shared an order of french fries. Jim and Angie split a piece of apple pie.

"You all read the book," Jim said. "What did you think about the movie?"

"Pretty close to the book," Nick said. "But they left out a few scenes."

Angie laughed. "Yeah. I wasn't sure how they were going to show that breast-feeding scene."

Ruth snorted, then turned serious. "I don't know. In a way I think the movie missed the point. It seemed overly optimistic."

Nick nodded. "Yeah. It was a bit too Hollywood for me. I mean the Joads end up in a camp with good food and indoor plumbing? Give me a break!"

Someone in back put a nickel in the jukebox. Soon, Glenn Miller's *Moonlight Serenade* filled the room. Everyone in the cozy booth remained quiet for quite a while until Ruth broke the silence. "So what are you boys doing at Fort Clatsop?" She asked.

"Mostly just marching around," Nick said, trying to give Ruth his most handsome smile.

Jim punched Nick lightly on the shoulder. "True enough. Marching around. But this guy's a sharpshooter. Going to be a great sniper."

"Cut it out, Jim," Nick said.

"No, really." Jim leaned over the table toward the girls. "He just missed sharpshooter by one point."

Ruth's smile soon faded into darkness. "Do you think we're going to get into this war?"

For several long moments, they remained silent, but the threat of war was on everyone's mind.

Jim was first to break the silence. "It looks to me we're going to end up in this war one way or the other."

"Not if those America First guys have anything to say about it," Nick said.

"I think those guys are naïve," Ruth said. "Don't they know staying out of it now will only bring those same wolves to our door one day?"

Angie shrugged. "I don't know. My Dad's a big cheese in the America First group here in Astoria. He believes we can stay out of the war and be safe. I'm not so sure. We try to avoid talking about politics at home."

"Hell. We can talk about it here, baby," Jim said with a gentle stroke of her cheek.

Nick didn't say much. He basically agreed with Ruth and Jim. But if war was coming, we sure as hell weren't ready for it.

A half moon shone brightly over the mouth of the Columbia River as Jim pulled the Ford over on a lonely stretch that overlooked a spit where the river met the ocean.

Jim and Angie were soon necking in the front seat. Nick, on the other hand, was a bit reticent. He was just getting to know Ruth. *But dang! She was one bang-up girl.*

"Have you ever been out here before?" Ruth asked.

Nick shook his head. "No. Just downtown Astoria."

"Do you like it here?"

Nick placed his hands gently on her shoulders. As she turned toward him, moonlight bathed her face. "It's *you* I like out here," he said with a soft kiss. After a moment's hesitation, she returned a passionate kiss.

1941

Chapter Four
Tora! Tora! Tora!

JAPAN RATTLES SWORD BUT ECHO IS PIANISSIMO—
over in Japan the sword rattling goes on with all sorts of threats and dire predictions of what will happen if the United States tries to tell Tokyo what to do; yet the echo in Washington does not hurt the eardrums. The Japanese spokesmen in the American capital wish to continue negotiations with the United States.

New York Times
December 7, 1941

Dufur, Oregon
December 7, 1941

The steady snowfall was beginning to accumulate in the corners of the attic window that looked out over glistening wheat fields toward Mount Hood. Ducking his head beneath the rafters, Nick walked carefully across the pine floorboards toward a pile of items covered with an old blanket beneath the eaves.

Early morning sunlight, muted by the light snowfall, illuminated the fine particles of dust shaken from the blanket as Nick pulled it aside. In the middle of a pile of books, 78s and a varsity sweater, was the football trophy he'd received his senior year. With its faux-golden figures corroded and peeling, the most outstanding player award seemed to be from a distant era. Most outstanding? What the hell does that mean? At right end, Jim got the most valuable player award. Not surprising really. Nobody pays much attention to the right guard. But we were both linemen, I guess. Nick ran his fingertip across the outstretched wings of a golden eagle mounted on the base of the trophy. Now my finger's on the trigger and Jim's feeding the ammunition belt. We're still a team.

"Nicky," his mother's cheerful voice rose up the ladder to the attic. "Better get ready for church."

With a loud flutter of its wings, a jet-black raven dislodged a puff of snow from the ridge of the roof above the frosty window. Nick watched as it lighted in the upper branches of a Douglas fir just past the barn.

Onward, Christian soldiers, marching as to war. With the cross of Jesus going on before! Belting out one of his favorite hymns, Nick glanced at his mother and father who were singing along with great gusto. On the aisle of their pew, Jim's older sister and her lanky husband swayed like windswept stalks of wheat along with the rhythmic energy of the congregation. Nick closed his eyes and let his voice soar. It was great to be home again.

As they filed out of the sanctuary, the minister grasped Nick's hand firmly. "Thanks for stepping up, Nick," he said. "I know you will do us proud." Nick nodded and walked out into a sunny and cold midday on the snow-covered plains south of the Columbia River. He always felt like an impostor when someone complimented him for simply being in uniform. But after church, shaking hands with the minister he'd known all of his nineteen years, Nick had little choice but to nod with a smile.

"Hungry?" His mother asked. "My icebox rolls are rising and the roast should be just about done when we get home."

"We've got jam, beans and potatoes in the truck, Mom," Nick's sister said. "I'll just need to reheat the vegetables a bit."

Nick licked his lips. He could taste it already. His mother always put together his favorite meal when he came home on leave. And the produce from his sister's farm here in the foothills of the Cascade Mountains was a veritable ripsnorter.

Before stepping into the backseat of his father's 1934 Buick sedan, Nick took a moment to inhale the clear, 38-degree air through his nostrils and observe a thin cirrus cloud trailing across the face of Mount Hood like a wispy, silk scarf. Nestled between the Cascade Mountains, Columbia River Gorge and the high desert, there was nowhere else like his hometown on a clear winter day.

Heading north on the Dalles-California Highway out of Dufur, cars and trucks began pulling over to the side of the road. There was no sign of an accident or roadblock.

"What's going on?" His father said.

Nick rolled down his window and squinted into the vehicles idling along the edge of the snowbank lining the road. "They seem to be tuning in to their radios."

Nick's mother snapped on the radio and tuned through static to the relatively strong signal of KEX in Portland. She increased the volume so everyone could hear.

This is a special news bulletin. President Rosevelt has announced that the Japanese have attacked Pearl Harbor Hawaii by air. The attack was also made on the principal island of Oahu. And just now comes word from the President's office that a second air attack has been reported on army and navy bases in Manila..."

Nick leaned over the front seat and put a firm hand on his father's shoulder. "I've got to get back to the post, Dad."

His father nodded and stepped on the accelerator pedal. After serving in the Great War, he knew about duty. "Will Jim Anderson be picking you up?"

"Yeah. I just need to throw a few things in my duffel bag."

Dumbfounded, everyone was silent for several minutes. Then Nick's mother spoke up. "Do you have to go tonight, Nicky? It's a long trip up to Fort Lewis. Couldn't you boys drive back in the morning?"

Nick shook his head. "No, Mom. In a national emergency we have to return to post on the double."

"Do you have enough gas?" His father said. "Long way to Tacoma."

"Don't worry, Dad. The tank's full and we also have a Jerry can."

"I just wish you didn't have to drive at night," his mother said.

Nick forced a smile. "We'll be fine, Mom. Stop worrying."

The setting sun glittered off the windshield of Jim's Ford sedan as they drove across the Columbia River Bridge into Washington State on Route 99, the Pacific Highway. With no snow here on the coastal side of the Cascades, the verdant landscape was cast in shadows. Far below the metallic green span of the bridge, red and black buoys tilted westward in the current of the mighty river coursing swiftly toward the open sea. Nick watched a tugboat heading downriver into the sunset. War? Sure, they'd been training at Fort Lewis for a year. But going into actual combat? It wasn't something he'd really imagined. He was only 19 years old. It would be great to be a hero. But what if he were killed?

Periodically, columns of olive drab jeeps and troop carriers with white stars emblazoned on their hoods sped by them as Jim drove steadily north. By the time they reached Longview, it was pitch dark. Along a narrow arm of the river, amber floodlights illuminated grain silos and lonely stacks of timber. The hazy light cast shadows against the hulls of two freighters lined up along the dock. Then only miles of darkness interrupted by the twinkling lights of small towns scattered along the way.

At Centralia they pulled off the highway beneath a tall Texaco sign with a red star on a white field. Atop a building shaped like a Pullman car, a weathered, neon sign with several letters barely illuminated, buzzed like a trapped bumblebee with the words *Pacific Highway Diner*. A long-haul trucker, kneeling to examine his rear axle, looked up as Jim and Nick passed by. "You boys heading into it?" Nick nodded. "Good luck. Get me some Japs."

Cigarette smoke, steam and the odor of burnt cooking grease filled the air as Nick pushed open the heavy metal door to the diner. With all the booths filled, Nick and Jim sat at the counter between a stocky trucker and a sailor. Beneath the anxious hubbub of customer's voices, the juke box throbbed with the Sons of the Pioneers. *All day I've faced the barren waste without the taste of water, cool water.*

"What'll it be, boys?" The counter man with thinning hair, rolled-up sleeves and a weary half-smile asked. Jim ordered coffee and a slice of apple pie. Nick asked for a hamburger with fries and a Coke. "Okey dokey," the man said. "Coming right up."

Jim looked at his watch. "We should make the post by midnight, don't you think?"

The lanky sailor sitting next to Nick leaned over. "You guys headed to Fort Lewis?"

"Yep," Nick said. "How about you?"

"Puget Sound Naval Yard in Bremerton. But the scuttlebutt is I'll be in Seattle soon."

"How come?" Nick asked.

"Transfer to Fort Lawton for embarkation."

Back on the road, neither Nick nor Jim spoke for quite a while.

"I guess we'll be heading to Fort Lawton too," Jim finally said.

"It's what we've been training for, isn't it?"

"Yeah, but I guess I never really..." Jim paused.

"Me neither," Nick said.

Jim thumped Nick's arm . "We'll be all right, buddy. Just need to pull together. That's all."

Childhood memories flashed through Nick's mind. Pulling together. That's what he and Jim had always done. Covering each other with alibis when needed. Helping each other with difficult homework assignments. Reassuring insecure girlfriends. Making a skilled assist instead of driving for the winning basket. They were a team. And now they were about to enter the biggest contest of their lives.

Nick watched the oncoming headlights wash over Jim's face as he drove along the highway. "We'll be okay, buddy," Nick said. "Everything's gonna be okay."

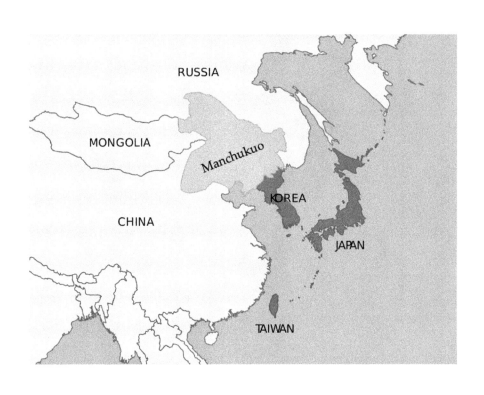

Chapter Five
Secret Camp

Ambassador Kichisaburo Nomura and Ambassador Saburu Kurusu left the American State Department Friday after their eighth official contact with Roosevelt administration leaders on the problems of the Pacific...indicating their determination to leave nothing undone to induce the United States to accept Japan's most reasonable terms for a settlement of pending differences.

Japan Times
December 7, 1941

Changbai Mountain Range
Southeastern Manchukuo
December 7, 1941

Maintaining firm traction on the Korean guerrilla's leg as Dr. Zhang sawed through the femur below a tourniquet, Ho-jun glanced up from the operating table at the window high on the wall. Large, silver snowflakes, glistening against the late afternoon sky, streamed past the window panes of the Northeast Anti-Japanese United Army (NAJUA) cabin like a silent waterfall. At the head of the table, the Chinese nurse Lì Xuě, whose given name meant lovely snow, titrated the

41

anesthesia by pouring small amounts of ether onto a cloth-covered wire frame that fit over the patient's mouth like a geodesic tent.

Ho-jun stretched his shoulder muscles and shifted his feet. Squeezing his eyes shut, he shook his head momentarily to one side like a dog emerging from a cold stream. No one noticed. It had been a hard week without much sleep. Pro-Japanese counterinsurgency forces sweeping the remote, forested regions of the Changbai Mountains had discovered several hidden camps of the NAJUA. The resulting battles had inflicted devastating losses on NAJUA forces. This small field hospital on the border between northeast Korea and Manchukuo was now overloaded with wounded Chinese and Korean NAJUA guerrillas in addition to a dozen soldiers with serious disorders such as pneumonia, tuberculosis and frostbite.

With a final, strong pull on the surgical saw, Dr. Zhang separated the femur, removed the remaining soft tissues with a scalpel and placed the severed leg in a bucket. Stepping away from the table, he turned toward Ho-jun. "Want to finish up, Ho-jun?" Ho-jun nodded. "Next time you can do the complete amputation," Dr. Zhang said with a weary smile.

With Dr. Zhang cutting the surgical knots, Ho-jun ligated the severed blood vessels and closed the wound. Lì Xuě removed the ether mask from the patient and dressed the wound with a compression bandage. Ho-jun released a long, deep breath. This should be the last procedure of the day. But with mounting casualties, no calm moment was certain.

Dr. Zhang spoke to a young Chinese corpsman who was dispensing medication to the patients lined up on mattresses against the wall like tattered leaves blown against a snow drift. "We're going to take a break, Yu. Is everything in order?" Yu nodded. Dr. Zhang looked about the cabin and raised an eyebrow. "Isn't corpsman Yang back yet?"

"He was supposed to be back this morning, Comrade Doctor," Yu said. "I hope he hasn't run into the *Gando* unit. They were spotted yesterday near Helong."

Ho-jun involuntarily tightened his jaw muscles. The dreaded, elite Manchukuo Imperial Army battalion composed mainly of ethnic Koreans, had become increasingly effective in eradicating NAJUA activity in the region. So feared were they, that eight young Korean girls had recently jumped to their deaths in an icy river rather than risk capture by the ruthless Gando force. Highly trained in anti-guerrilla tactics and generously supplied by the Japanese with equipment, rewards for successful operations and funds to bribe defecting guerrillas, the Gando Special Force was on the brink of driving the NAJUA entirely out of Manchukuo.

As Dr. Zhang sat down to record his operative note, Ho-jun pulled a heavy, fur-lined coat over his quilted, winter uniform. "I think I need some fresh air before rounds. Would you like to join me?" He asked Lì Xuě.

Outside the cabin the late afternoon temperature had dropped to minus 10 degrees C and the snowfall had lightened to a whispering murmur. An occasional gust of wind launched diaphanous, white puffs from the snow-layered branches of spruce and pine trees that lined the steep slopes of the ravine encircling the camp. Gray smoke spiraling from the chimneys of two wooden barracks and the field hospital blended with the falling snow and soon dispersed into the dense forest.

Bundled in her heavy winter jacket and canvas fleece mittens, Lí Xúe's delicate face was framed by the fur-lined hood. Rays of ebbing sunlight, filtering through the forest like amber ribbons of muted gold, highlighted her high cheekbones. Ho-jun thought she was one of the most beautiful women he'd ever known. Additionally, she was a skilled nurse with several years of combat experience. Calm and soft-spoken, Lí Xúe had proven a godsend for a recent medical school graduate with little knowledge of clinical practice.

Ho-jun lit two Japanese *Kinshi* cigarettes and handed one to Lí Xúe. "What do you think his chances are?" He asked.

Lí Xúe's cigarette smoke billowed into a white cloud as it diffused into the veil of softly falling snow. "I don't know," she said. "The wound was pretty clean. He may do well—if we can keep it from being infected." She paused. "Of course, with no sulfa drugs that's an open question. But don't worry, Comrade Doctor. I'll keep a close eye on it."

Ho-jun briefly closed his eyes and nodded. Lí Xúe was a dream nurse—beautiful, smart and extremely competent. And she always seemed prepared to support or defend him. Maybe after the war they might find a life together. Wait. He didn't even know if she liked him. He turned toward her, and looked directly into her eyes. "Ready for rounds, Comrade nurse?"

Back on the ward, Ho-jun and Lí Xúe examined a Chinese soldier who was delirious and sweating profusely. As Ho-jun gently palpated his abdomen, the patient cried out in pain.

"How did he do last night?" Ho-jun asked.

Lí Xúe frowned as she opened the patient's chart. "Chills and fever. Confused. A nosebleed and bloody stool this morning."

Ho-jun stroked his chin. "Could be typhus or typhoid. Any headache or respiratory complaints?"

Lí Xúe consulted her nursing notes. "He's been delirious, so it's hard to say about headache. There's been a little dry cough, but no tachypnea. Blood-pressure at noon was 90/70. Pulse 110. But take a look at this." She handed him a chart of the patient's vital signs.

Ho-jun perused the chart. The patient had a step ladder temperature rise to 40.5 degrees C. But simultaneous pulse measurements never rose above 85. Ho-jun pulled up the patient's shirt and scrutinized his chest. Pressing his fingertips against a rose colored spot on the patient's dark skin, he held the pressure for a few seconds, then released it. The spot never blanched.

Ho-jun looked at Lí Xúe.

She nodded. "Typhoid fever."

1942

Chapter Six
Blood and Snow

Five years have elapsed since the China Affair broke out. But Japan still holds to the idea that China is Japan's brother country. There has been no change at all in Japan's desire to embrace China into its great but warm arms and look after it with tender care. In spite of this, Chungking has kept up its stubborn resistance for more than four years. During the intervening period this country has often advised it to reconsider its bigoted attitude, but it has failed to act upon our warm-hearted advice. To make matters worse, Chungking has continued to rely upon the United States and Britain.

> Premier Hideki Tojo
> Japan Times
> January 24, 1942

Changbai Mountain Range
Southeastern Manchukuo
January 24, 1942

Ho-jun rose from his thick *yo* floor mat around midnight, grabbed his boots and tiptoed between the rows of snoring soldiers to the heavy wooden door of the military barracks.

Pulling on his boots and fur-lined coat, he lifted the latch and stepped into the frigid, midnight air.

Snow glissaded down through evergreen branches and bitterly cold air coursed through Ho-jun's nostrils like an icy mountain stream. He scanned the steep, forested slopes surrounding the camp for enemy activity. Nothing. Only the wondrous silence of moonlight and the shimmering stars high above the mountains. *Hoo hoo hooo* sang an owl hidden among the snow-layered trees.

Ho-jun stepped onto the meter-deep, snow-packed path that ran between the barracks and the hospital. Each footfall crunched beneath his heavy boots; each exhalation hung in the glacial air like smoke trailing a determined locomotive on an uphill slope. Moonlight, glinting off the pure-white crystals of fresh snow, sparked his desire. Lí Xúe was awaiting their midnight tryst.

Except for the usual snoring, the hospital ward was quiet, and the corpsman Yu was fast asleep in a corner. Ho-jun removed his boots and stepped onto the ladder leading to the loft where Lí Xúe slept alone. A sinking creak pierced the silence as the first step of the aging, pine ladder sagged beneath his weight. Ho-jun scanned the ward. No one stirred. Gingerly, he measured each step with gentle pressure and continued up to the loft like a stealthy Korean *Hwarang* warrior.

On the top step he paused. Moonlight, streaming through a single window beneath the rafters, cast a silver curtain over Lí Xúe, lying beneath several heavy blankets in a dark, narrow space between stacks of medical supplies. The pleasant scent of burning embers from the wood stove below permeated the chilly atmosphere.

For several long moments Ho-jun studied her face. Her glossy, raven hair cascading across the burlap bag she used for a pillow. Her effortless breathing, deep and rhythmic. Shadows cast by her nose and brow in the moonlight shimmered across her cheeks. Ho-jun had to catch his breath. Was this beautiful creature actually in love with him?

Lí Xúe stirred as Ho-jun took off his coat and boots and slid under the blankets behind her. Reaching back, she laid a hand upon his thigh and whispered in low and dusky Mandarin *"Wǒ de àirén"*—my beloved. She rubbed her eyes. "I'm sorry I fell asleep waiting for you. I was exhausted after all the admissions today."

Ho-jun molded himself against her, his pelvis against her lower back, face buried in her soft hair, lips kissing the nape of her neck.

Lí Xúe turned to face him and held his head in both hands. "I always want to be with you, Ho-jun." She paused, then smiled. "You'll like Mukden. It's a lovely city. My family would be delighted to have us. And Dr. Zhang already offered us jobs at the hospital." She sighed. "After this war of course…"

A loud, splintering sound shot up the stairs as the hospital door below flew open and crashed against the wall. Then the orderly Yu yelling. *Did you bring them here, Yang?* A burst of machine gun fire. Screams of patients being bayoneted on their mats.

Ho-jun met the first enemy soldier at the top step of the ladder to the loft. Although wearing Imperial Japanese Army

51

winter gear, it was obvious   the enemy was Korean—the *Gando Special Force*. Ho-jun kicked the invader in the head with the heel of his stockinged foot and flung him to the floor five meters below. As he raised his foot to strike the second man coming up the ladder, the man grasped Ho-jun's other ankle and wrestled him to the floor. More special force soldiers swarmed up the ladder, seized Ho-jun and hurled him off the loft like a sack of rice.

Ho-jun had no idea how long he'd been unconscious. The first of his senses to return was hearing. Someone calling his name in the distance. Then intense pain in his shoulder. He slowly opened his eyes and tried to clear his head.

Dr. Zhang's face was close to his. "Wake up, Ho-jun! We've got to escape now. Everyone here is dead. The Gando force is attacking the barracks. But they'll be back to see if anyone's still alive."

Ho-jun was becoming alert. Smoke drifted across the floor. He looked up at the loft just as the burning roof collapsed with a shower of sparks. "Lí Xúe!" Ho-jun struggled to stand.

Dr. Zhang held him back. "It's no use, Ho-jun. She was dead long before the fire began." Ho-jun sank back to the floor. Dr. Zhang bowed his head. "I'm sorry."

Dr. Zhang grabbed a heavy winter coat hanging on the wall and a pair of boots left by the door. "Get these on!"

When Ho-jun fumbled, Dr. Zhang took over and quickly dressed him for the bitterly cold night. When the heavy coat was pulled over his left shoulder, Ho-jun winced. "That's where you fell," Dr. Zhang said. "No time to splint it now." He grabbed his medical kit. "Let's go!"

Ho-jun cradled his left elbow with his right hand as he scurried behind Dr. Zhang out of the burning hospital toward the forest. Screams, punctuated by intermittent gunfire, erupted from the burning barracks only 50 meters away.

Just as he was about to enter the relative safety of the forest, a snapping twig froze Ho-jun in his tracks. Dr. Zhang kept running. Emerging from the shadows behind the hospital like a stealthy wolf, was a tall man in the winter uniform of an officer in the Imperial Japanese Army. Yellow-orange light from the burning buildings flashed across his rugged face, delineating a thick scar that ran from his lip to chin like a craggy mountain range. *Mapsosa!* It was his old friend Kwang-min.

Eyes riveted on each other's faces, neither of the men spoke a word. Kwang-min calmly lit a cigarette and exhaled a cloud of smoke that curled upward in the icy-blue moonlight. Then shouts and curses as a Korean squad of Gando Force soldiers swarmed around the corner of the building. Kwang-min jerked his head to one side in a silent message. *Run you fool.* Ho-jun darted into the dark woods and raced from tree to tree as the Gando Force opened fire. After several blind volleys into the forest, Kwang-min commanded his men to cease-fire.

Dr. Zhang and Ho-jun ran through the woods, heading down the mountains toward the Yalu River. At 0400 they stopped and listened carefully. With no sign of a search party in pursuit, they needed a short rest. Dr. Zhang burrowed into the snow beneath a large Sitka spruce as Ho-jun gathered brush for a makeshift roof and cave lining. After packing snow on a roof fashioned from overlapping pine branches, they lined the shelter with bushy spruce to keep their bodies from conducting heat directly into the snow.

Dr. Zhang tried to assess Ho-jun's shoulder injury. But, since any movement elicited great pain, he simply fashioned a sling with gauze rolls from the medical kit. "Splinting's the best treatment for now," Dr. Zhang said. "Even if something's broken." With a grimace, Ho-jun nodded. He knew what he had to do. Keep it splinted. Keep moving. Hope it doesn't get worse.

Ho-jun lay back against the spruce branches. His whole body ached. His mind hyper-vigilant like a Siberian tiger on the run. His heart shattered to pieces. What happened to Lí Xúe? Dr. Zhang would only say that she was already dead when he arrived at the hospital. A sharp pain caught his breath. *Gaesaekki!* Sons of bitches. Had those traitorous Koreans of the Gando Forces raped her before they killed her? Did she suffer? Dr. Zhang couldn't say. He only knew she was dead. But how did the scene appear? Dr. Zhang said he couldn't remember. Overwhelmed and exhausted, Ho-jun fell into deep, disconsolate sleep.

In an arduous, two-day descent through the mountainous forest, Ho-jun and Dr. Zhang survived with only melted snow for sustenance. At the northern arc of the Tumen River on the border between Korea and Manchukuo they separated. Dr. Zhang headed west on a dangerous journey through Japanese-occupied territory to join resistance forces near his home in Mukden. Ho-jun continued southeast toward the Soviet administrative territory of Primorsky Krai.

Clinging to the far eastern border between Manchukuo and Korea like a great bear, Primorsky Krai was the home of the Soviet Pacific Fleet on the Sea of Japan. Although the relationship between the Soviet Union and its traditional enemy Japan was tenuous, the two nations were not at war with one another in 1942. With Japanese success in eradicating significant resistance throughout occupied China, many Chinese and Korean anti-Japanese guerrillas were fleeing into Primorsky Krai.

Eyes half-closed and limbs aching, Ho-jun trudged south along the banks of the Tumen River toward the Soviet border. Gusts of glacial wind propelled clouds of crystalline powder across the glistening, crusted snow. Each arduous step crunched the snow deep beneath his boots. Everything was lost—his country, his best friend and the love of his life.

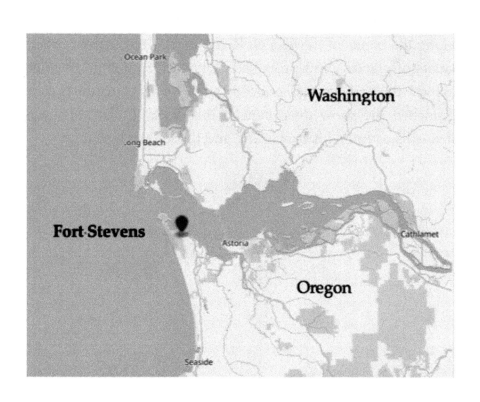

Chapter Seven
Defending the Coast

A WEST COAST PORT—*Fifty-three survivors of an American merchant vessel torpedoed at 2:10 p.m. Sunday by an enemy submarine off the North Pacific Coast were landed here today after being rescued by a fishing vessel and a corvette.*

Los Angeles Times
June 10, 1942

Fort Stevens, Oregon
June 21, 1942

On Sunday afternoon the coastal sky was clear as blue crystal with a light wind and temperature a comfortable 65 degrees F. After a year of advanced combat training at Fort Lewis, this assignment to the old gun battery at the mouth of the Columbia River was far less rigorous, but anticlimactic for Nick who was hoping to see action soon after the attack on Pearl Harbor.

On the upside, Nick's assignment to Fort Stevens put him a stone's throw away from the home of Ruth Taylor, the lovely girl he'd dated back in the summer of 1940. She sure was a doll. Although they'd lost touch when he was transferred up to the Puget Sound, they were now making up for lost time.

While other units of the federalized Northwest National Guard had already departed for the Pacific War, Nick and Jim were among the 2500 men assigned to this post-Civil War era fort as America prepared for a possible Japanese invasion of the West Coast.

Built in 1865, Fort Stevens was one of three artillery batteries arrayed on the Oregon and Washington sides of the Columbia River as it emptied into the Pacific Ocean. The fort was armed with 10-inch, rifled cannons mounted on disappearing carriages that hid the guns behind concrete walls like predators waiting to rise to the attack. Complementing the vanishing cannons, were mortar and small caliber rifle batteries.

Nick and Jim were assigned to a team of thirty-five men at Battery Russell, the only gun emplacement that faced the Pacific Ocean. Armed with two disappearing cannons, the battery could fire a 600-pound shell every minute with an effective range of eight miles. Although they fired the cannons each month for practice, most of Nick's time was spent drilling, marching, on lookout duty or polishing the battery's equipment and ammunition.

Fort Stevens was a boring assignment, particularly now, six months into the war, when a Japanese invasion of the West Coast was becoming increasingly unlikely. When Nick and others expressed their desire to see some action in the Pacific, their grizzled Top Sergeant Kowalski (SGT K), a veteran of the Great War, could only mutter: *be careful what you wish for, boys.*

With no assigned duties at the fort on Sunday afternoon, Nick was riding his friend Jim's Schwinn Roadster bicycle into the town of Hammond to visit Ruth. Nick was falling in love.

It wasn't just her lustrous, brown hair, sparkling blue eyes and nice figure—Ruth was whip smart and had a vivacious personality. Home after her sophomore year at Oregon State College in Corvallis, Ruth was excited about her major in education.

After a mile on the paved Pacific Drive, lined with scattered pine trees and flowering Scotch Broom, Nick turned on to a bumpy, gravel lane that passed by fisherman's shacks and wooden fences draped with emerald-colored nets drying in the sun. Passing through a grove of alders, he arrived at the Taylor place on the Columbia River estuary.

A rocky beach with a narrow stretch of sand lay just behind the house which was built on a rise above the bay. Beside the house, the open doors of a weather-beaten barn released odors of oil and sawdust into the salty ocean air. Scattered on the dirt floor inside the barn, rust-flaked tools clustered around a marine engine on blocks, and stacks of wiry, crab pots rising high along the walls. Nick shielded his eyes from the brilliant, afternoon light reflecting off a row of windows on the upper floor of the Taylor home. There she was! In the faint shadows of the front porch, Ruth was sitting in a swing that hung between the beams.

Nick leaned the bicycle against a scraggly, shore pine and walked up to the house on a gravel path lined with rhododendrons. A gentle breeze just barely stirred a wind chime into a soft, high-pitched ding. Just before the front steps, a deep-red, rock rose hedge delineated a small victory garden of zucchini, tomatoes, green beans and lettuce.

Ruth rose from the swing, smiling and fresh in a green, cotton dress and saddle shoes. Her satiny hair was pulled back on one side and held with a silver clasp. Nick felt the urge to pinch himself. *She looked good enough to eat.* He skipped up the steps and embraced her on the landing with all his might. Her lithe body melted into his arms as he nuzzled his face through her hair and murmured "I've missed you."

"Hello, Nick!" boomed a deep voice behind the partially open front door. A burly man with a weather-beaten face stepped into the sunlight. Nick extended his hand into the vise-like grasp of Ruth's father. "Good evening, Mr. Taylor."

The older man smiled. "How are things going at the post, son? Keeping the Japs off the beach?"

"Yes, Sir. So far so good."

"Now what are you two up to today?"

"It's a big minus tide, Daddy," Ruth said. "We thought we'd bike down to Delaura Beach and find some razor clams."

"Bring me back some." Mr. Taylor said and ambled like a black bear back into the house.

It was a great day for a bicycle ride together. The fields were still green from recent rain and only a few wispy clouds drifted across the sky. At Delaura Beach Nick and Ruth leaned their bicycles against a gnarled driftwood stump and walked through dune grass to the shore. A minus 1.2 tide exposed packed sand far out to sea. Empty crab shells, fractured sand dollars and diaphanous jellyfish lay widely scattered on the sand.

Along the water's edge, a flock of seagulls nestled into their feathers against the breeze. Offshore, a dozen brown pelicans dipped and soared just above the water like aerobatic pilots in tight formation. Although familiar to Ruth, it all seemed exotic to Nick.

Along the tide line they pressed their boots beside dime-sized holes in the sand made by razor clams. Nothing. Nothing. Then squirt! A small stream of water shot up by Nick's foot. He plunged his shovel straight down a few inches on the ocean side of the hole. Crunch!

"Darn!" Nick muttered as he deposited part of a razor clam's mahogany shell and its torn body on the sand. "I'm just a rookie at this. Nowhere as good as you."

"They dig straight down about a foot every 30 seconds," Ruth said, pointing out another clam show. "Try this." She plunged her shovel into the sand with the aplomb of a skilled clammer. "Wriggle the handle back and forth before you take out the wedge."

Soon a healthy squirt of water erupted by Ruth's foot, and she quickly performed the maneuver she'd just described. This time there was no crunch. Up with the sand came a fully intact, five-inch long, razor clam, retracting its thick, rubbery neck. "Yay!" Ruth crowed, tossing the clam into the bucket.

After a few more dismal attempts, Nick finally mastered the maneuver. Before long, they had more than a dozen clams in their bucket.

The sun was dipping into the western horizon as Nick and Ruth came back through the kitchen door of the Taylor home. Mrs. Taylor, a slim woman with sturdy, brown shoes and graying hair tied in a bun at the back of her neck, was standing at the kitchen counter preparing dinner. "Hello Nick," she said with a smile. "Looks like you two dug up some real hors d'oeuvres for dinner."

Ruth and Nick dumped the clams into the sink and rinsed them with cold water. Ruth showed Nick how to open the shells with a knife edge without cutting your finger. Then butterfly the siphon and foot and cut away the gut. Bread them with cornmeal, flour, salt and pepper and fry them in a skillet with a thin layer of butter.

After everyone in the kitchen had one, Mrs. Taylor handed Nick a plate. "Why don't you put the rest of the clams on here and take them out to the men? We women will finish up here in the kitchen." Ruth smiled and nudged Nick through the swinging kitchen door.

With the Astorian Evening Budget newspaper draped across his knees, Mr. Taylor was filling his pipe with Briggs tobacco. Twelve-year-old Johnny, rangy in a plaid shirt and slacks, sprawled on the rug perusing a Daisy Red Ryder BB gun ad in a Batman comic. "It's only $2.95, Dad."

Nick held out the plate. "Try one of these beauties, sir."

Mr. Taylor grasped a warm razor clam between his fingers and motioned Nick to sit on the sofa. Johnny reached up and snared a clam for himself.

"Been a good crabbing season, sir?" Nick asked.

"Yup. Pretty good. Haven't pulled up any mines yet!" He laughed.

"Are you gonna get to shoot the cannons?" Johnny asked.

"Polish, stack shells and drill every day. That's what I do. Haven't shot 'em off though," Nick said.

"Well, I'm glad you're there, son. To protect us," Mr. Taylor said.

"To tell the truth, sir, I'd rather be fighting out in the Pacific."

Mr. Taylor leaned toward Nick, his muscular forearms taut, his expression abruptly somber. "I wouldn't be too eager, son," he almost whispered. "Not as glorious as it looks in the newsreels."

Nick looked directly into Mr. Taylor's eyes. "You were in the Great War, weren't you, sir?"

"Yep," Mr. Taylor said. "The war to end all wars." His face darkened, then looked sad.

Nick was unsure what to say. Most people, outraged by Japanese attacks against America, were jumping on the martial bandwagon. What had happened to Mr. Taylor in the Great War?

"Come and get it!" Ruth yelled.

Bowls and platters of corn, beans, bread and meatloaf lay on the dining room table that was covered with white linen. Mrs. Taylor and her husband sat at opposite ends of the table and folded their hands. Mr. Taylor said grace. "*Come Lord Jesus be our guest and let these gifts to us be blessed. Amen.*"

Glassware clinked and silver scraped against porcelain. "Have some." "Thank you." "Here you go." Then a lull in the conversation as everyone took a first bite.

Johnny broke the focus on the meal. "Mom, do you think we really need to do the blackout every night?"

Mrs. Taylor chuckled. "I must admit the blackout seems a bit silly. I hardly think the Japs will bomb Warrenton."

"Also, our scoutmaster said everyone should have emergency stuff like blankets and food at home," Johnny said.

"Your scoutmaster's right," Mrs. Taylor said. "We should have something laid up. But it's just hard right now with only 28 ration stamps left for the year."

Ruth turned to her mother. "What happened to Mr. Okomoto's fruit stand? I didn't see it on the highway today."

Mrs. Taylor sighed. "I heard the whole family was resettled in Utah. A sad thing really. Such a nice family, the Okamotos."

Mr. Taylor placed both hands on the table and shook his head. "I guess there were some real problems though. Jap spies going up and down the coast like tourists taking pictures."

"Well, maybe," Ruth said. "But do you think we really should put all the Japanese who live here in camps, Daddy?"

Don't go there with your dad, Nick thought. He shifted his weight and turned toward Mr. Taylor. "Well, they certainly have a toehold now, don't you think, sir? Up in the Aleutians I mean."

Mrs. Taylor stood and laid a hand on her husbands arm. "Pretty far away isn't it, dear? Almost to Japan and so cold. Not much they can do up there, do you think, dear?"

Mr. Taylor stroked her soft wrist with his weathered hands. "Yeah. Pretty far away. Don't you worry now, sweetheart."

Mrs. Taylor pushed away from the table and stood up. "Who'd like some marionberry cobbler? I used quite a few sugar coupons to make it."

The cobbler was delicious, and the rest of the dinner table conversation was light as gentle rain on a summer day. When Mrs. Taylor began pulling the drapes across the dining room windows for the blackout, Nick realized it was time to say goodbye. After one last delicious kiss with Ruth on the front porch, he began peddling back to the post.

Out on the highway, an occasional automobile passed by, its half-blackened headlights beamed downward toward the dark pavement so no light escaped into the night sky. In sync with the rhythmic chirping of crickets deep in the woods, Nick began to hum softly. *Chattanooga Choo Choo, won't you choo choo me home?*

A lone sentry waved Nick on through the gate of Fort Stevens. With a lot of men on leave, the post was dark and quiet. Both the movie theater and the canteen had closed for the night. Several flashlights flickered like fireflies as men sat in the darkness reading or writing letters. The muted tones of Glenn Miller wafted from the main barracks. *Couple of jiggers of moonlight and add a star.*

Inside the barracks, dark curtains were drawn over the windows in accordance with the dim-out. Several card games were still going, but most of the soldiers lay on their bunks reading or talking with one another.

Jim, on his bunk reading *The Moon is Down* by John Steinbeck, looked up. "How'd it go, Nick?"

Nick smiled. "Swell. Ruth is a dreamboat. And I learned how to clam." He gestured toward the book. "That any good?"

"Well, not as good as *The Grapes of Wrath*," Jim said. "But interesting. He doesn't actually say it, but the enemy soldiers are obviously German."

"A different kind of war against the Krauts, I guess," Nick said. "We've got a lot in common. But the Japs are pretty different, don't you think?"

Jim grunted in agreement and resumed reading. Nick took his Gibson guitar from beneath his bunk, gritted his teeth and began tuning the high E string cautiously. Since breaking the last one a few days ago, he had no more replacements. Placing his ear against the body of the guitar, he practiced changing chords. It didn't take him long to fall asleep. It'd been a great day.

A little before midnight, the sound of an explosion jolted Nick out of deep sleep. Men were running outside the barracks as a bugle sounded the call to arms. "What's going on?" Nick shouted at Jim.

"Don't know," Jim yelled, scrambling out of his bunk. "Sounded like a bomb."

"Man your posts!" SGT K. yelled through the barracks door. Someone snapped on the lights. Half-awake, Nick and the other soldiers stumbled about, pulling on their clothes, and hurriedly lacing up their boots.

There was a decrescendo whistle, silence, then a loud explosion somewhere south of the drill field. The sounds repeated at short intervals with no discernible pattern. Shells seemed to be landing close, but no obvious damage could be seen.

"Flashes in the sky several miles out!" The sentry shouted from the guard tower.

"Lights out!" The Lieutenant yelled through the barracks door as he ran toward the gun battery. "Don't give them a target!"

Nick and his fellow crew members ran like gazelles across the field and through the brush to the artillery station at Battery Russell. In the dark, Nick stumbled over a concrete marker in front of the battery. Clutching his helmet in his hands, he fell face first into the gravel. Quickly rising to his knees, he touched his forehead. Blood trickled between his fingers.

He ran into the magazine deep within the concrete battery and manned his position at the ammunition pile beneath a platform holding the huge cannon. The Lieutenant looked at Nick's bloody face. "Are you wounded, soldier?"

"No, sir. Just fell in the gravel. I'm okay."

"Well, get a medic to give you a bandage. I don't want you bleeding all over the ammunition."

Another whistle, pause and explosion shook the ground. Nick's hands trembled. His pulse bounded more with excitement than fear. A strange feeling of detachment came over him. This was surreal. They were actually under attack, maybe being invaded. He ran out of the gun battery across the field to the aid station where a medic applied a bandage to his forehead. "We'll clean it up later," the medic said, and sent him back to his post.

"We're ready to fire, Sir," SGT K. called out from the platform above Nick's head as the 36-ton recoil weights were locked into position.

The Lieutenant frowned. "Hang on, Sergeant. We have no orders yet. I'm going to check with the Captain."

Jim shook his head as the Lieutenant ran off to the command post. "I don't like just sitting here taking this incoming crap without a fight," he grumbled. "What're we waiting for? To be blown to smithereens?"

"No orders yet. Just hang on," SGT K. barked down at the ammunition team. Then, muttering to himself, he added, "Damn fools need to make a decision."

Another explosion. Still a bit to the south. It seemed the ordinance was being walked northward up the beach. Nick wiped blood-tinged sweat from his forehead with the back of his hand. Damn! Why the hell don't we fire back?

A searchlight on the guard tower began to scan the ocean, but it was shortly extinguished by order of the Harbor Defense Command. Without the searchlight, plotters tried to use the intermittent flashes of gunfire from the vessel to calculate its range. A series of estimates yielded conflicting data. Some calculations indicated it was within firing range, while others estimated it was too far out to sea.

The Lieutenant returned to the battery. "We're not going to fire, men. It's a sub. Must have snuck in through the minefields with the fishing boats."

SGT K. snorted, slapping his forehead with his hand. "What the hell, Sir! Can't we at least give it a try?"

The Lieutenant shrugged. "She's too far out, Sergeant. Estimated 20,000 yards. This old gun can't reach much beyond 15,000. We'd only give them a nice bright target to zero in on."

Orange bursts flashed across the horizon followed seconds later by whistles and booms. Occasionally there was a flash without any sound, an apparent dud. The shells came at odd intervals, landing unpredictably around the post.

It only lasted 20 minutes, but it seemed like eternity to Nick. The random shelling, the impotence of not responding, and the fear that the next one might land on top of him, dragged out each minute. About midnight, the bugler played two long notes and the word was passed down the line—all clear.

"Some of those sounded awful close," Nick said while walking back to the barracks with Jim.

Jim shook his head. "What the hell were they doing? Just trying to scare us?"

Brushing aside an undergrowth of salal, they stepped into a clearing. Nick halted Jim with a hand on his chest. "Son of a bitch! Look at that!"

On the baseball diamond next to the drill field, a fallen power line sparked and buzzed like a hornet trapped in a glass jar. A crater ten feet wide had erased home plate and reduced the old backstop to a tangle of wire and splintered wood.

1944

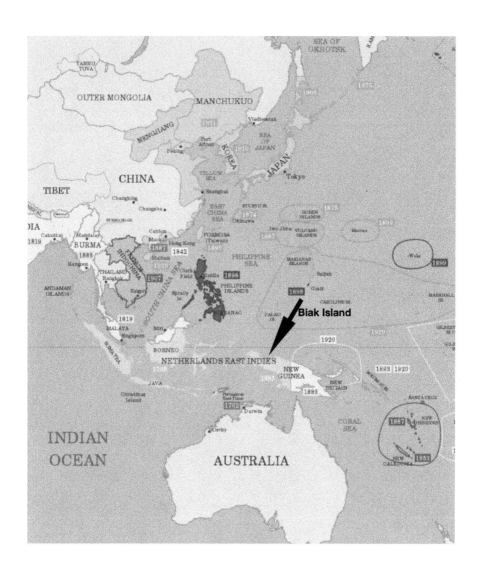

Chapter Eight
Sands of New Guinea

BIAK ISLAND—*Our attack planes bombed and strafed enemy installations from Mokmer to Sorido. Defense positions were hit and a coastal vessel was sunk offshore.*

New York Times
May 25, 1944

Biak Island, New Guinea
May 27,1944

Wham! Sergeant Nick Jackson and his ten-man machine gun squad flung themselves onto the beach moments before an explosion showered them with grains of pure-white sand. The Japanese mortar team in the palm grove above the beachhead was zeroing in.

Spread across the shore like a wrack line at high tide, Nick's squad and the other 180 men of Charlie Company bristled with M1 Garand and Browning automatic rifles, Tommy guns, trench mortars, machine guns and flamethrowers. Some had scrawled *Fight!* or *To hell with Tojo!* across the back of their field jackets. Officers and medics, however, wore no insignia at all since Japanese snipers would always target red crosses and any insignia indicating rank.

Nick brushed his fingers across the trigger guard of his rifle. The cool touch of steel and walnut flooded him with memories of his unit's recent combat on Wakde Island—hand-to-hand fighting against Japanese soldiers hidden in spider holes, coconut log bunkers and coral caves. It had been a vicious fight to the death with over 400 Americans and 6000 Japanese soldiers killed. Still, Nick remained unscathed. Was there really only one Japanese bullet with his name on it?

With barely a breather after securing Wakde, General MacArthur ordered Nick's infantry regiment into the amphibious assault on Biak, a 948-square-mile island with three Japanese airfields at the northwest tip of New Guinea. Taking the airbases on Biak could tip the balance in western New Guinea and tighten the ring around the mighty, Japanese fortress of Rabaul on New Britain Island. The mission on Biak was to dislodge the Imperial Japanese Army from the island and continue the inexorable, but costly, advance up the coast of New Guinea.

Nick and his friend Sergeant Jim Anderson each led a machine gun squad in a platoon commanded by an inexperienced shavetail Lieutenant. Fortunately, the seasoned First Sergeant K was second in command. At dawn, their Landing Craft Infantry (LCI) boat, affectionately named *Elsie*, had nosed over the coral onto Biak's south beach, exactly as planned. But the following LCIs were taken off course by a strong ocean current and disembarked far from the landing zone. Charlie Company was isolated on a narrow stretch of sand between the ocean and a palm grove.

Another mortar shell burst nearby. Nick pressed his forehead into the sand and pulled the steel rim of his helmet back over his neck. Although he'd seen a lot of combat since landing down the coast at Finschhafen in March, he was always on edge at the start of a battle. It wasn't just the flashes and explosions, nor the zip of bullets kicking up sand all around him. He knew he'd soon face a fierce and determined enemy in mortal combat.

Nick's heart pounded, his jaw clenched tight as a vise. He had to get focused. Fixing his eyes on the mortar and machine gun flashes from the palm grove, he raised his rifle and aligned its sights. With both eyes open, he relaxed his arms and shoulders and took deep breath. As he exhaled, he gently squeezed the trigger. After a few rounds, he stopped firing. There was no change in enemy fire. He'd wait for a clear target.

Japanese mortar fire continued to pockmark the beach, sending great clumps of sand high in the air before falling on Charlie Company like sheets of golden rain. Hazy, blue smoke, permeated with diesel and creosote fumes, wafted over the beach as the mortar fire steadily advanced across the men lying flat on the sand. They couldn't stay here much longer. All eyes were on the young Lieutenant, waiting for the signal to attack the grove.

The Lieutenant rose, pumped his rifle in the air and blew his whistle three times. "All right, men! Let's give 'em hell!" Before he could take a step, a burst of machine gun fire cut him down.

Nick was stunned. The Lieutenant had been a popular leader for a shave tail. Just this morning he'd fired up the men with his confidence and enthusiasm. Now he was gone. Just like that.

The diesel engines of the LCI roared as it backed off the beach, spewing smoke and foam. With mortars exploding all around them and machine guns chattering from the palm grove, First Sergeant K. assumed command of Charlie Company. "Everybody move out on the double! Dig in just behind the sand dune."

Nick rose to a crouch and picked up the machine gun spare parts box and water can. *Dat dat dat.* Two Japanese machine guns flashed from the palm trees 200 yards inland. With bullets kicking up sand all around him, Nick sprinted in a zigzag pattern toward the relative shelter of the rising dune. Time slowed down—*he was returning a punt on a crisp fall day in front of the home crowd. Cleats digging in to the lime-striped turf. Pivoting and darting away from defenders.*

Halfway to the dune, a low-flying Mitsubishi Zero appeared out of nowhere to strafe the beach. Yellow tracers zipped across the path of two men carrying ammunition boxes behind Nick. Nick froze in mid-stride and turned. Neither man was moving. Blood pooled around the head of one and the other's legs were wildly twisted and bent.

SGT K. yelled at him. "They're dead, man! Move out!"

Nick resumed his sprint through the hail of enemy fire from the palm grove toward the dune where most of his platoon had hurled themselves down. He heard the Zero banking for another run. 100 yards to go. Too far. An image of Ruth flashed through his mind. What a life they could have had.

Then, roaring just above the water, two twin-boomed, P-38 fighters blazed over the beach. Although the P-38s chased the Zero away, the mortar and machine gun fire from the grove was unrelenting. Nick hurled himself against the base of the dune.

Jim crawled over dragging an ammunition box. "Christ. We nearly bought the farm this time. You okay?"

Nick looked back at his dead comrades lying on the sand. "Yeah sure. Let's set up."

Jim crawled back down the line to his machine gun squad as Nick's team got to work. The gunner and his assistant cut an arc in the sand dune and set the heavy Browning machine gun on its tripod. Zip! Zip! Japanese bullets chipped away at the top of the dune.

The assistant gunner inserted an ammunition belt into the feed pawl and lowered the extractor over the first round. The gunner released the firing pin and glanced at Nick. Nick thumped his shoulder twice, and the gunner began raking the grove with 30-caliber fire. The second machine gun squad under Jim's command was also firing as SGT K. crawled down the line between the two squads. He glanced at Nick with apparent approval and moved on.

A high-pitched ringing in Nick's ears enveloped the staccato machine gun, thudding mortar and crackling rifle fire. He crouched behind the dune and focused his binoculars on the palm grove. The naval barrage laid down just before the attack had trimmed the tops off most of the palm trees. Tattered fronds dangled from their splintered trunks. Shell craters, fallen trees and piles of scrub vegetation dotted the smoky landscape.

It was difficult to see the hidden Japanese positions, but it seemed there were only a few machine guns and mortars. No detectable infantry so far. From his experience on Wakde, Nick knew the Japanese infantry often held back, waiting to spring a surprise counterattack at the right moment. This was probably just a superficial line of defense along the beach. Still, he knew they wouldn't withdraw. That's the way these monkeys like to do it—set up small skirmishing forces to slow you down with no plans for retreat. You just have to run over them. And that always cost a lot.

American rifle squads poured fire into the grove as their trench mortar teams began to find their range. After ten minutes of heavy pounding, there was no Japanese return fire. Two squads of men with rifles and flamethrowers slipped over the dune and advanced cautiously. Just before they reached the grove, a single shot rang out from behind a tangle of fallen palm trees. An American rifleman crumpled to the ground. A hail of American rifle fire and the sweep of flamethrowers silenced any further resistance and all units advanced into the smoking palm grove.

Nick looked into the Japanese machine gun emplacement hidden behind a stack of palm logs. The gunner and his assistant lay sprawled in a trench, one without an apparent scratch, the other in a bloodstained shirt. In front of them a perfectly intact Nambu Type 92 heavy machine gun sat on its tripod.

Jim examined the Nambu. "So this is the *woodpecker*, eh?" He spat on the ground. "Damned if it didn't sound like one though."

Nick gestured toward the dead Japanese machine gun crew. "Stupid bastards. Dying for the Emperor? Just like always. We take a blood bath and they all die. Jesus."

SGT K. told the platoon to take a breather in the grove before moving out. Nick and Jim leaned against the coarse layered bark of a once-sturdy palm tree. Tattered leaves, smoldering branches and broken coconut shells littered the ground around them. Nick fished a Lucky from his shirt pocket and flicked open his Zippo. Jim dug out his own preferred Pall Malls and cupped his hands around the lighter. With deep drags and slow exhalations, they sat in silence.

Nick traced a finger over the radiant orange sun set on a red and blue field etched on his Zippo. "The *Sunset Division*. That's what we are, right Jim? Not MacArthur's goddam *Jungleers*."

"Sunset. Does that have a good connotation like beauty?" Jim said. "Or is it ominous, like the end of the road?"

Nick laughed. "Still the optimist, I see."

Everyone in Charlie Company knew this was just the first act. Intelligence, albeit a bit sketchy of late, forecast many obstacles between them and the main airfield including dense jungle, swamps and high coral ridges, honeycombed with caves. But one thing at a time. First came a 100-yard open field, dotted with scrub vegetation, that lay between the palm grove and a mangrove swamp.

SGT K. knelt down on one knee beside them. "I just talked with the Captain. Here's the skinny." He began drawing in the sand with the tip of his Ka-Bar knife. "Our platoon heads straight north through the swamp." He plunged the 7-inch blade into the sand. "Here! The rest of the company will split in two parts, advancing wide on our flanks. We'll meet up on the other side and regroup before attacking the ridge above the airfield." He paused and wrinkled his brow. "Our boys did well so far. Losses pretty light. Any questions?"

Nick and Jim shook their heads. SGT K. reached down and took a drag off Nick's cigarette. Springing up, he stretched his arms behind his back and surveyed the terrain. "Okay, boys. Let's move out!"

A single rifle shot crackled from the mangroves on the other side of the clearing. With a look of bewilderment, SGT K. clasped a hand to his neck. A stream of blood pulsed between his fingers as he fell backward into a tangled pile of palm fronds.

The platoon poured blind, angry rifle fire into the mangroves while Nick and Jim knelt beside their fallen top Sergeant. His eyes were open and his face lacked any expression. Nick felt for a pulse. Nothing. "Cease firing! Everybody hit the dirt!" He yelled.

Jim rose up on his elbows to survey the situation. Zip zip. The sand flew up beside him. He quickly flattened out. "Christ, Nick. Lieutenant and Top both went down. Looks like you've got the platoon now. What's our next move?"

Nick considered the options. With the rest of the company moving wide on either side of them, their platoon was on its own. The field between the palm grove and the swamp was 100 yards wide with a few fallen trees and patches of scrub brush. They'd be completely exposed to enemy fire unless they had some cover. It would take too long to get any air support for such a small mission, and he didn't want to request a naval salvo in close quarters. He'd seen it come down on their own heads before. He looked at Jim and cocked his head. "We're just going to have to make a run for it. Take your boys to the right. I'll go left."

Nick's shirt stuck to his back in the intense, midmorning sun as he lay in the palm grove, surveying the field before them. Probably full of ticks and poisonous snakes. Hell, worry about them later. First the Japs. This is not the main force we're up against. They're hanging back somewhere waiting to spring a trap. Still, there'll be snipers and machine guns just waiting for us to make a move. He looked up at the clear blue sky. Who do I send out on point? Maybe to their deaths?

"Higgins, take the point. Riccardi and Johnson, flank him. Machine gun crews, set up here 50 feet apart to cover us. Everyone else keep low, 20 feet apart in a V formation. I want three M18 smoke grenades about 20 yards out in front. On my command."

The two machine guns began raking the mangroves, starting low then moving high enough to clear their own advancing men. On Nick's signal, the smoke grenades were thrown and 20 men began running, bent low at the waist. One-two-three. Zigzag to the left. One-two-three. Right. Bits of dirt flew in the air from sniper fire. A single machine gun rattled from the mangroves. Both American machine guns swung about, focusing their fire on flashes of light bursting between two twisted mangrove trunks.

Higgins and Riccardi were hit before reaching the cover of the red smoke. Blind enemy fire continued as the Americans raced on through. With live grenades in hand, they emerged into 50 feet of open space before the grove. Johnson went down just as he was about to throw his grenade and it exploded a few feet from his body. But several other grenades found their mark and the enemy machine gun was silenced.

Holding their weapons in firing position, Nick's platoon entered the swamp cautiously. Each step in the shallow, muddy water required an extra effort to free their boots from suction as they maneuvered through tangled vines, shrubs and flowers that twisted about the massive roots of the towering mangroves. Most direct sunlight and any hint of an ocean breeze was filtered out by the dense canopy of the trees. Heavy, humid air dampened all sound and the powerful odor of rotting vegetation filled their nostrils.

Nick and Jim crouched behind a large rust colored log several yards into the swamp. Jim gestured back toward the open field. "Should we send the medic out to check on those guys?"

"Got any bead at all on those snipers?"

"Hard to say for sure. I think there're only two." Jim pointed to a group of trees covered with tangled vines and large dense leaves. "One's somewhere up in there. I think the other one's right in front of us."

Nick called the medic over. "Doc, we've still got our machine guns covering from the palm grove and I'm putting our best marksmen on a couple of sites where we think the snipers are. Think you can make it out there?"

Without hesitation, the medic grabbed his kit. "No problem, Sarge. I'm ready when you are."

The medic raced out into the field and knelt down by Johnson. His shirt was soaked with blood. No carotid pulse. The medic shook his head. Suddenly, a clump of dirt flew up by his foot, followed instantly by a crackling sound from the trees.

"There!" Jim pointed and a fusillade of American rifle fire stripped leaves and bark from a fork high up in a mangrove tree. A uniformed figure fell into the lower branches and one of Nick's men began sloshing through the water toward the tree.

"Hold it!" Nick held up his hand. "Why didn't his rifle fall? Remember what they did on Wakde."

Nick scanned the thicket around the fallen figure with his binoculars The branches in an adjacent tree rustled slightly. Then he saw the thin rope stretching between the two trees. "That's a dummy!" He pointed to the second tree. "Sniper's over there!"

This time the concentrated fire of a dozen riflemen had the right target. A long-barreled rifle with a telescopic sight tumbled down through the branches and landed in the mud at the foot of the tree. Above, a khaki-clad figure, shrouded in a vest of palm fronds, dangled from a rope tied around his waist. His face and hands were painted forest green.

The medic raced on to Higgins and Riccardi. Nick scanned the trees. Why is there no opposing fire? Is the second sniper waiting until our backs are turned? The medic gave a thumbs-down gesture. All three point men dead. Jesus!

Nick spoke calmly to the riflemen who had brought down the first sniper. "Find that second Nip bastard. He's not far away."

It didn't take them long. As Jim had predicted, the second sniper was perched in a tree just in front of them. He got off one glancing shot that ricocheted off the side of a GI's helmet before he was brought down by intense M1 and BAR fire. Nick posted a few men on the perimeter and brought in the machine gun crews from the other side of the field. Ordering everyone to take a break, he slogged over to the fallen sniper's tree. He picked up the Japanese rifle and wiped the mud off with his sleeve. Etched in front of the bolt was a 16-petal chrysanthemum, the imperial seal of Japan.

A private came over to take a look. "An Arisaka 97. Pretty standard issue. Good souvenir though. Right, Sarge?"

Nick handed him the rifle. "Got no time for souvenirs. It's yours if you can carry it."

The battle for the ridge above the airfield lasted almost two days. Three hundred Japanese soldiers, ensconced inside large caves connected by tunnels 75 feet underground, refused to yield easily. Automatic weapons, flamethrowers and air strikes had little effect. American losses were high. Finally, after gasoline was poured into the crevices around the caves and ignited, resistance faltered. According to a captured Japanese soldier, their Major burned the regimental flag and ordered his troops to attempt an escape. The wounded were instructed to kill themselves with hand grenades. Then, the Major committed *seppuku,* ritual suicide. Most of the 100 men trying to escape were cut down as they scrambled out of the caves. Only six Japanese prisoners were taken.

Nick and the 15 survivors of his 28-man platoon reached the top of the ridge in early evening. Unable to dig trenches in the hard surface, they piled chunks of limestone and coral around themselves for fortification. Lying on a tarp spread over the rocky ground, Nick watched clouds of acrid smoke from the smoldering caves drift across the ridge. The smell of cordite, gasoline and burnt flesh filled the air. The Army graves registration unit picked up the American dead, and any useful equipment was removed from the battlefield. But dead Japanese soldiers lay scattered where they fell midst their smoldering weapons and equipment.

It was unusually quiet. Some men read letters or gazed at faded photographs. A few cleaned and oiled their weapons or sharpened their bayonets. Nick lay with his head resting on his helmet, puffing a cigarette that burned close to his fingertips. As the sun dipped low on the horizon, a welcome light breeze picked up. It was the first break in the relentless, scorching heat since they'd landed on Biak.

An aid station was set up next to the command post in the center of the defensive circle. Medics quickly triaged the wounded into three categories: those needing immediate attention, those that could wait a while, and a few who appeared to be beyond available medical help. Large bore needles poured plasma and morphine into heavily bandaged men as they lay on stretchers awaiting evacuation. Despite a few moans, the sweetness of morphine seemed to calm most of the wounded. Those who were able to sit, just smoked and waited. The dying who were still conscious, lay silently, staring upward.

Nick watched a lone cumulus cloud traverse the clear blue sky. *Funny about the wounded.* The medics treated them with great tenderness, but now they were clearly different from the rest. They'd be going back to a different world. Some to New Caledonia or Australia. The most serious ones, back to the States. Nick released a sigh. It was hard to imagine going back to the real world. And Ruth seemed to be further and further away.

Jim put the last piece of limestone in place around their shallow enclosure, flopped down next to Nick and tore open a carton of Ten-in-One rations brought up from the rear. For the first time in days, there was the possibility of a warm meal.

"Hold it," Nick said, pointing to a group of soldiers who were opening a Japanese pack. "Let's see what those guys have to trade."

They walked over to a group of soldiers who were sitting around a makeshift foxhole radio. One was examining the Japanese rations.

"What you got for some tins of beef stew and peaches?" Nick asked.

"How about rice and a can of salmon?"

"Done," Jim said, exchanging the items. "What's on the radio?"

"Zero Hour's just beginning," said the radioman.

"Oh great," Nick said. "Tokyo Rose always has some bad news we haven't heard before."

"I just like the music," said a young GI.

"Well, you guys enjoy it," Jim said. "Come on, Nick. Let's eat."

Nick poured the whole bag of rice in his canteen cup, added some water and began boiling it over the small, portable cooking stove that came with the Ten-in-Ones. Nick and Jim caught globs of sticky rice that steamed over the edge of the cup and stuffed them in their mouths along with pieces of salmon.

"Not bad actually," Jim mumbled between bites. "Hell. The Japs eat better than we do."

"Yeah. When they've got it. But you saw those guys. They've been looking pretty thin since we cut off their supply line."

They sat silently for a while, munching their meal and quaffing water from their canteens. Jim picked up his pack. "Guess it's time for our atabrine cocktails."

"Okay, Mom," Nick smiled and took a huge yellow tablet from his pack. He swallowed the anti-malarial pill with a large slug of water to dilute the retchingly-bitter taste of the atabrine. He held up his yellowed palms. "Pretty soon you won't be able to tell us from the Japs."

Jim thumped him on the shoulder. "You said it, brother. You're going more Asian every day."

The last rays of the sun were disappearing on the horizon and the sky was turning gray. Since the Japanese often tried to infiltrate the lines at night, defensive positions were arranged in a circle 50 yards in diameter. On the perimeter, machine guns were placed 20 yards apart to afford a scissoring pattern of fire. But no one wanted to shoot, since a flash of gunfire would give away your position to any Jap crawling through the bushes. Then all he had to do was toss a grenade. Still, when sounds were heard, a challenge and response were required. Tonight's password, *Laura's lover*, took advantage of the difficulty Japanese had pronouncing Ls and Rs.

Nick and Jim lay with their heads on their helmets, silently watching the stars emerge in the sky. Compared to what they were used to, there were many more bright stars here in the southern hemisphere.

"Wow! That Milky Way is a lollapalooza!" Jim said. "A lot brighter than Oregon, eh?"

"Yeah," Nick said. "But you know, I miss the night sky in Oregon. Seems like yesterday we were out with the girls in Astoria. The National Guard sounded great, didn't it? Couple hours a week in The Dalles and two weeks on the coast every summer. A small price to pay for a few extra bucks."

Jim chuckled. "Who'd have guessed we'd get nationalized before our time was up? Fucking war hadn't even started yet!"

"Well, things weren't too bad in Australia. We had some good R&R at the beach, didn't we?"

Jim sat up abruptly. "Look at that!" They silently watched a falling star streak across the sky.

"Of course everything changed when we got here," Nick said.

"New Guinea. End of the earth, buddy."

Down below the ridge a flare shot up in the sky, then drifted slowly downward, casting sparkling, white light over a dark palm grove near the airfield. Distant rifle and machine gun fire erupted sporadically from a hillside to the North. After several minutes of exchanging fire, it was quiet again.

Jim stretched out and Nick took the first watch. He looked up at the twinkling stars. He'd get back to Ruth somehow. He just had to keep remembering that.

Thirty minutes into his watch, Nick briefly nodded off a few times. He straightened up, shrugged his shoulders and refocused his attention on the perimeter. A faint rustling sound snapped him to full attention. He released the safety on his M1 and scrutinized the shadows cast by starlight across the scrub vegetation and jagged rock formations. Maybe it's a land crab or one of those whistling tarantulas. They like to come out at night. There it was again! A scraping sound on rocky soil. He nudged Jim awake and gestured with a tilt of his head toward the direction of the sound. Jim sat up quickly and grabbed his rifle.

Nick issued the challenge. "Halt! Who goes there?"

"Don't worry. It's just me, Joe," a soft voice replied.

The next few moments seemed to pass in slow motion. The pineapple-shaped, hand grenade skipped off a piece of limestone and fell to the ground between them. Jim's wide-open eyes met Nick's for the longest moment. They both reached out, but Jim got there first. Before he could throw the grenade back toward the Jap, it exploded in his hand. A surge of blood-red light flooded Nick's consciousness, then a field of tiny, sparkling stars against a pitch-black sky.

Chapter Nine
88th Special Rifle Brigade

Having outflanked and wiped out the forces of Gen.Tang En-po by a brisk development of three dimensional warfare in the steep mountain passes of the Funiushan range, the Japanese are now pushing irresistibly onward to Luoyang, the ancient capital of the heart of China.

Nippon Times
May 27, 1944

Vyatskoye, Khabarovsk Krai
Union of Soviet Socialist Republics
May 27, 1944

Under shimmering stars on a moonless night, Ho-jun increased his pace on the path beside the coursing Amur River. Swollen from a week of steady rain, the river was surging through town, an impatient force slapping against the rocks along its banks. The constant roar of the river and the clear evening air embraced Ho-jun with the sweet ache of early spring as he hurried to meet Alena. Maybe her mother knew about their clandestine affair—Alena was never sure. But if her father found out there would definitely be trouble.

In 1937, concerned that some were Japanese spies, the Soviet regime relocated all ethnic Koreans living in far-eastern Russia to central Asia. The presence of Ho-jun's 200-man rifle brigade, composed entirely of Koreans, was a jolt for this quiet, Russian fishing village. But the Soviet army recognized the value of seasoned guerrillas who'd fought with the Chinese Communists in Manchukuo. Under the command of Soviet Army Major Kim Il-Sung, a former NAJUA officer, the Korean soldiers composed the 88th Special Rifle Brigade.

Aside from a few border skirmishes, no major hostilities between the Soviet Union and Imperial Japan had broken out in 1944. Nevertheless, the neutrality pact they'd signed in 1941 was now quite fragile. In Vyatskoye the Koreans of the 88th Special Rifle Brigade received advanced training in military tactics along with instruction in the Russian language and communist ideology. A few of the Koreans with exceptional Japanese language skills were trained as translators.

As medical officer for the brigade, Ho-jun's duties included routine sick call, response to rare emergencies and compulsory attendance at daily military and political lectures. Weekends were usually free, but uneventful. That is until Alena came to work in the clinic. Now, secretly in love, they found it best to meet only in the deepest night when her hard-working parents were fast asleep. Every Saturday after midnight, Alena awaited Ho-jun in a small clearing in the forest behind her family's wooden cabin.

Starlight sparkled off the golden dome of the Orthodox Church across the pulsing river as Ho-jun strode along, humming softly to himself—*Arirang, arirang, arariyo.* After four years marching with the guerrillas in Manchukuo, the tune frequently emerged whenever he walked alone. The 600-year-old song had become the anthem of Korean resistance against Imperial Japanese rule. It was a song of longing and loss. But it was also the legend of a young man and a maiden who fell in love while picking camellias on opposite banks of a rushing river. In one version of the story, the young man drowns as he tries to swim across the river. In another, they remain apart, forever longing for union.

On the edge of town, Ho-jun turned off the path and entered a dense forest of pine, oak and birch trees. Soon, the sound of rustling leaves and a soft whisper floated through the darkness. *"Lyubov moya.* Over here, my love." Alena's voice emerged from a small clearing.

Ho-jun strode forward and swept her into his arms. *"Lyubov moya,"* he said trying his best to pronounce the Russian words, so unlike Korean. His fingertips glided down her thick, golden plait, across her lower back and along her thighs. "I've missed you," he murmured, his lips nuzzling her neck.

The sweet, musty scent of pine sap drifted in the forest air as they lay in the cool grass, their backs against a moss-covered trunk of a fallen oak tree. Ho-jun kissed her softly, then deeper as their breaths rose with increasing passion. Alena pressed her body against his and parted her lips. His tongue swept back and forth across hers as his fingertips probed beneath her cotton blouse. Alena pulled the blouse free from her skirt, allowing him to caress her full, round breasts beneath the soft fabric of her undershirt. Ho-jun traced a fingertip back and forth across the waist of her skirt until Elena brushed it away. Pressing a hand against his chest, she gently lifted his chin with the loving reminder they'd agreed not to have intercourse before marriage. "We have a lifetime ahead of us, Ho-jun."

Ho-jun leaned his head back, looking up at the stars glittering in the charcoal sky. "There we are," he said, wrapping his arm around her. "Jupiter and Saturn. The two brightest objects in the night."

Alena pressed against him. "We're sparkling diamonds."

"Ahh. I like that." He kissed her. "You're quite the poet."

Alena laughed. "Actually I'm not. That's from Chekhov."

Ho-jun was deeply in love with Alena. Despite the obstacles of war, his rudimentary Russian language skills and cultural restrictions, he would marry this woman. But the timing had to be right. For now, this is how it had to be.

Time slowed down as they snuggled together beneath the stars, dreaming of the future they would have together. Then, with the first glimmer of pink light in the eastern sky, Alena rose. "I've got to get home. My father will soon be up to fish for the Kaluga."

Ho-jun didn't complete morning sick call until noon and, with only two hours of sleep, his energy was beginning to fade like a marathoner in the final mile. But there was no time for a nap. Major Alexei Konikov was always punctual with his afternoon political ideology class. His Korean language skills were surprisingly good, albeit accented with the typical rolled back tongue of the Russian language.

"Who was the father of communism?" The robust Major Konikov asked, fixing his intense gaze on a rugged Korean soldier sitting on a bench in the back row.

The soldier bit his lip and furrowed his brow. "Karl Marx?"

"Correct," the Soviet instructor said with a brisk nod. He looked around the barracks at the assembly of former Korean guerrillas, now dressed in the dark, khaki uniforms and tall, black boots of the Soviet Army. "What did Marx write?"

"The Communist Manifesto," a soldier sang out.

"Along with Friedrich Engels," Ho-jun added from the front row.

"Correct, Comrade Choi," Major Konikov said with a slight smile. "And what did the Manifesto say?"

"It said class struggle has existed in every society throughout history and capitalism makes our world dangerously unstable."

"Yes!" Major Konikov declared, looking into the hesitant, weather-beaten faces of men who have known only war. "That's why our great leaders, Comrades Lenin and Stalin, have created a society where all property is publicly owned and every worker is paid according to his abilities and needs." He stood tall. "That's all for today, comrades. Dismissed."

Benches scraped and leather boots clomped across the dusty floor as the men exited the barracks in respectful silence. Major Konikov unbuttoned his uniform jacket, shook out two *Belomorkanals* cigarettes from a crumpled pack and handed one to Ho-jun. "So, you've been reading Marx, Ho-jun? I'm surprised you have the time between your duties and love life."

Ho-jun compressed the hollow, cardboard extension of the cigarette between his fingers to form two flat surfaces and placed it between his lips. Major Konikov lit them up with a petrol lighter emblazoned with a hammer and sickle embedded in a red star.

"Actually," Ho-jun said. "Having grown up in a society ruled by the *Yangban* elite, I find Marx intriguing." He looked his Russian friend straight in the eyes. "But does it work, Alexei?"

Alexei chuckled. "You shouldn't try to stare down a Russian bear, Comrade." He leaned in and lowered his voice. "I'll admit we have a way to go, my friend. But I can tell you, life in the Soviet Union is much better than it was under the Czar."

"Anything would be better for Koreans than living under the heel of Japan. So I'm interested in your ideas, Alexei."

"Excellent. I'll make a good communist of you yet." Alexei placed a hand on Ho-jun's shoulder. "How are things with Alena?"

"I have two lives with her, Alexei. A professional one in the clinic and another late at night. I wish both could be out in the open."

"I'm sorry, Comrade. But I can't see another option. This village won't accept your relationship with her. What are your plans?"

"I'd like to take Alena back to Korea. But it depends on how this war goes. Japan still controls most of East Asia."

"Don't worry, Ho-jun. Once we finish with the Germans in Western Europe, the Red Army will join the fight against Japan."

June 3, 1944

During the week, the secret lovers Ho-jun and Alena worked happily together in the clinic. But on Saturday night, when Ho-jun went for their midnight tryst in the forest, she never arrived. Only after several inquiries in town by his friend Alexei, did he learn what happened. Alena was caught sneaking out of her house late at night. Alarmed and angry, her father sent her far away to live with relatives. A dark wave swept Ho-jun out into a sea of deep sorrow. How many times must he lose true love?

1945

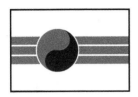

Chapter Ten
A New Nation

Kim, the Korean communist, opined that the new government of Korea must not and will not depend on help from the Central Communist Party in Moscow but that it must be governed on a broad and wide basis embodying the socialist and democratic ideals of all the Allied Powers. It must not, however, be patterned on either the Russian or the American system of government he added.

Nippon Times
October 5, 1945

Pyongyang, Democratic Republic of Korea (DPRK)
October 14, 1945

A constant, deep roar, undulating like the ocean, floated across the Girimi Stadium on Sunday as over 70,000 exuberant Koreans gathered to celebrate the liberation of their homeland from half a century of Imperial Japanese domination. Ho-jun and Alexei, dapper in their freshly laundered Soviet Army uniforms, sat behind a row of dignitaries arrayed across the stage. Although both their officer caps bore a hammer and sickle within a red star, each had distinct coloration, like the plumage of two proud birds. The green band and red piping of Ho-jun's Medical Corps visor was parrot-like. The magenta band and piping atop Alexei's cap was reminiscent of a hummingbird.

The energy of this raucous, flag-waving crowd pulsed through Ho-jun's body, reminding him of 1936, the last time he'd been in this stadium. It had been the annual title match between football clubs from Seoul and Pyongyang. The crowd became so agitated that officials had to stop the game several times due to rioting between rival fans. But there was no animosity in the crowd today, only pure gratitude for those who had finally broken the chains of Japanese imperialism. This was the long-awaited emancipation from tyranny; and hopefully, after a period of Soviet occupation, the rebirth of a sovereign nation.

Absorbing the joyful clamor of the crowd, Ho-jun floated on a pulsing cloud of euphoria. After five, anguished years in Manchuria and Russia, it was wonderful to be home again on a fall day, under clear skies with a seemingly bright future.

Alexei, sitting ramrod straight beside Ho-jun, also seemed mesmerized by the electricity of the crowd. What a good friend he'd become. A graduate of Moscow State University with specialized training in communist ideology and the Korean language at the Lenin Political Military Academy, Alexei was in every way Ho-jun's intellectual match. After years serving with patriotic, but relatively uneducated, Chinese and Korean guerrillas, it was a pleasure to form a friendship with a stimulating individual. But what Ho-jun liked most about Alexei was his genuine warmth, sense of humor and earnest beliefs.

Mansei! Ten thousand years. The crowd echoed the patriotic cry of the 1919 independence movement when over a million Koreans rose across the country to protest Japanese colonial domination of their homeland. Although the Japanese ruthlessly crushed the uprising, the cry continued to echo within the souls of Korean nationalists throughout the century.

Despite the intoxicating jubilation that saturated the air, Ho-jun felt a heaviness in his chest. Mansei had also been the secret password of his underground, student movement in Seoul. Doleful images flashed through his mind. The fresh, earnest face of his nursing student friend Sun-ja, killed by the Kempetai in Seoul. Lí Xúe murdered in Manchukuo by the Gando Special Force led by his own childhood friend Kwang-min.

Ho-jun exhaled through pursed lips. At times it felt simply overwhelming. His raw pain was matched only by what Koreans call *han*—a feeling of deep sorrow, resentment and anger.

Alexei placed a hand on Ho-jun's forearm. "Quite a day, Comrade . I fully understand your emotion."

The crowd hushed as the stocky, Colonel General Terentii Shtykov, Commander of the Soviet army occupation forces, thumped the balky microphone, sending a raspy, high-pitched squeal across the stadium. "Comrades! Thank you for your warm welcome of the Red Army in Pyongyang. As liberators, we look forward to the establishment of a free, democratic Korea. And now, it is my great pleasure to introduce a genuine Korean patriot Cho Man-sik."

Alexei leaned in close to Ho-jun's ear with the familiarity of a trusted and perceptive raven. "Cho's the one we wanted to lead the country," he said in a low voice. "But he refuses to accept the plan for gradual independence. He wants it now. That's why we chose Kim Il-Sung."

60-year-old Cho Man-sik, short haired with arched eyebrows and a pencil mustache, stepped up to the microphone and gazed into the throng. *"Mansei!"* He cried.

The crowd erupted like a dormant volcano, blasting swaths of pent-up emotion throughout the atmosphere of the stadium. Cho stood silently at the podium, a proud, patriot grandfather of the nation, periodically bowing toward the incessantly cheering crowd. After several long minutes, Cho stepped back to the microphone and proceeded with the introduction of Kim Il-Sung.

"As chairman of the local branch of the Committee for the Preparation of Korean Independence, I'm pleased to introduce a courageous guerrilla fighter who, as a Soviet Army Major, became liberator extraordinaire of our country—Kim Il-Sung."

Ho-jun and Alexei nodded politely, exchanging impenetrable half-smiles with one another as they applauded. They both knew Kim well. As a field doctor for the guerrillas, serving under Kim in both Manchukuo and Russia, Ho-jun found him competent and fair-minded. Alexei, the political officer for the 88th Rifle Battalion in Russia, also felt Kim had been a capable unit commander.

But their half-smiles indicated another concern Alexei and Ho-jun shared—the mythologizing of Kim as "the great leader" of the anti-Japanese resistance in Manchukuo. They both knew that, although a competent leader of the Korean guerrillas, Kim had been subordinate to the Chinese leaders of the NAJUA. And for the last three years Kim had been in

Russia, not in Manchukuo fighting the Japanese. Nevertheless, as the senior Soviet political officer in Korea, it was Alexei who was assigned to develop the myth of Kim the great liberator and compose his rousing speeches.

Kim Il-Sung, rosy-cheeked and slightly plump in his Soviet army uniform, stepped up to the microphone, eyes beaming like an Amur leopard emerging from the dense North Korean forest. The crowd murmured with cautious uncertainty. How could this baby-faced, young man be the intrepid guerrilla who led the fight against the Imperial Japanese Army in Manchukuo? And what claims to leadership did he have over thousands of other resistance fighters?

Raising his arm, Kim spoke emphatically into the microphone. "Eternal glory to the great Soviet army that liberated the Korean people from the yoke of the Japanese militarists. Now we must unite across all sections of society to build a new democratic Korea!"

Amid loud cheers, many in the crowd exchanged quizzical glances. Where was Kim from? After living in China and Russia for most of his adult life, Kim's accent was difficult to place. The Russian team, led by Alexei, helped Kim with his poor or forgotten grammatical skills in the Korean language. But the accent was something he would have to adapt himself.

When the cheers finally ebbed, Kim concluded in a resounding voice. "Let those with strength give strength. Let those with knowledge give knowledge. Let those with money give money. All people who truly love their country, their nation and democracy must unite closely in a sovereign democratic state!"

Although he appeared young, overweight and soft, Ho-jun could see what Kim Il-Sung did have. Charisma.

At twilight, like salmon swimming upstream in the golden light, Ho-jun and Alexei wove their way through the huge crowd leaving Girimi Stadium. Soon they were walking alone on a path through a deep-green forest of red pines intermingled with small groves of oak trees whose marcescent leaves had turned a brilliant, copper color. The rays of the setting sun filtering through the trees illuminated a saffron path through the pine-scented forest. Ho-jun was filled with childhood memories. How many times had he walked through *Moranbong* park on the way to school, the stadium, or the gymnasium? After five turbulent years away, it was like a dream to walk on this familiar path again.

Ho-jun and Alexei crossed over an ancient stone bridge, and ascended a steep, stone stairway to the top of the hill. After pausing a few moments to catch their breath, Ho-jun led Alexei through a grove of tall, thin pines to a rocky lookout that afforded a partial view of the city of Pyongyang. The lights of the city below were beginning to shimmer like fireflies on a summer evening.

Ho-jun was silent. The refreshing odor of terpenes radiating from the pine sap transported him into a reverie. This had been his favorite meditation place growing up. Now old memories came surging back like a powerful breaker cresting a jetty. When was the last time he stood here? Was it back in 1940 on the way to the White Swan to meet Kwang-min?"

The downhill path led to a field on the edge of the city, dotted with recently harvested, rice sheaves. Past a few scattered shacks and outbuildings, they emerged from a copse of barberry shrubs to an avenue lined with telephone poles, merchant signs and small shops. An olive-green streetcar, sparks showering from its overhead wire like scintillating raindrops, rumbled by as Ho-jun and Alexei turned onto a narrow side street.

On Sunday evening only an occasional pedestrian passed by the few rickety bicycles leaning against lamp posts along the street. The White Swan restaurant, a Hanok style building with semi-circular roof tiles and weather-beaten, pine siding sat in the middle of the block. Ho-jun and Alexei pushed through the wooden door of the restaurant and removed their hats, coats and shoes in the vestibule. Aside from clanking dishes in the kitchen and the low murmurs of a handful of patrons, the White Swan was quiet. A smiling waitress in hanbok dress led them to a table in the corner that was partially screened from others by an intricate, latticework divider.

Ho-jun scanned the restaurant. The familiar atmosphere had not changed since his last time here with Kwang-min. Antique kitchen utensils, peasant hats and farm implements hung on the wall. The rafters were lined with small ceramic bowls and ancient *kimchi* pots. Ho-jun was glad he'd brought Alexei to his favorite restaurant.

After the second round of potent, rice soju, the waitress served sweet, garlicky, barbecued beef *Bulgogi* and *Kimchi* cabbage soaked in ginger, garlic and chili brine. Side dishes included pan-fried mushrooms in sesame oil and strips of fried tofu.

"How did you think Kim did with your speech?" Ho-jun asked.

Alexei quaffed a small cup of chilled soju. "He certainly energized the crowd." He smiled sheepishly. "But I am a bit concerned about the heroic myth I've been composing for him.
"

"Myths do impart power, my friend. We'll see how he wields it."

Alexei turned somber. "That's why I'm concerned about Kim's move to oust Cho Man-sik. It looks like the old patriot will be the first to fall."

Ho-jun looked around the room. No one was close enough to eavesdrop. "Isn't that what your Comrade Stalin did with his purge in the 1930s?"

Alexei raised an eyebrow, then spoke in a very low voice. "Sometimes muscle is necessary, Ho-jun," he said with a weary smile. "I've had to learn how to keep my balance over the years."

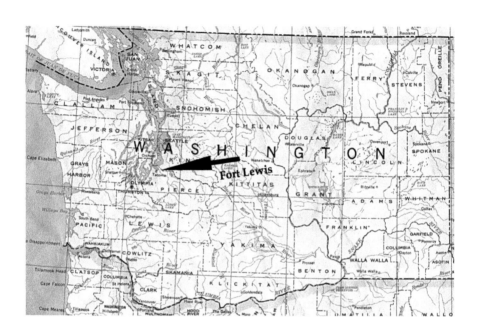

Chapter Eleven
Fort Lewis

WASHINGTON—*the heaviest passenger traffic load in the country's history will jam railroads and airlines for the rest of this month as troops pour in from overseas, as other servicemen shift to and from distribution centers and civilians crowd stations for a long Christmas weekend, the Office of Defense Transportation predicted today.*

New York Times
December 15, 1945

Fort Lewis, Washington
December 21, 1945

At 1730 Nick felt buoyant in his new PF-Flyers, as he navigated the familiar trail inside the perimeter of Fort Lewis. While he danced around puddles and mud holes like a nimble punt returner, his woolen fatigues and green, hooded sweatshirt held up like a mallard's plumage in the light, winter rain. Hardly wet, he brushed pearly raindrops from his sleeves. There was plenty of time for a good run. His wife Ruth didn't expect him home until 1900.

After his left leg had been severely damaged by a Japanese hand grenade a year and a half ago, the army surgeons had put Nick back together pretty well. Now, after a long hospitalization and six-months of intensive strength and endurance training, he was beginning to feel like his old self again.

It was his wife Ruth that concerned Nick the most. Following the devastating loss of her sister earlier this year, she had become silent and withdrawn. In May, her sister Emma, a minister's wife in southern Oregon, had gone on a Sunday picnic in the mountains with a youth group. When one of the teens pulled on a wire hanging down from a strange balloon lodged in a tree, an explosion killed them all.

Nick dodged a fallen branch and skirted the mud puddle beside it. *Christ. The Japs sent balloon bombs across the Pacific!* Such a pointless loss in the last months of the goddam war. They'd postponed the wedding until the fall. But even then, the celebration was very subdued.

By Christmas time, Ruth was beginning to rebound as she immersed herself in her work teaching undergraduates in the College of Puget Sound School of Education. Nick felt Ruth was doing OK. But still not fully back to her old self. He tried to tread lightly. Not push her too much. Let her come around on her own time. Be supportive, not critical. We'll get through this.

Nick set a moderate pace, focusing on the bracing, winter air that was filtering through the pines like mountain water coursing through a rocky stream. Coordinating his foot strike to land alternately on his right and left foot, he inhaled for three strides and exhaled for two—*in* 1, 2,3 and *out* 1,2. Never exhaling continually on the same foot. This rhythmic breathing technique, taught to him by a psychologist during his rehabilitation at Madigan Hospital, was intended to improve his running stability but also clear his mind.

To clear his mind. That's what Nick really wanted. But how could he stop reliving the war? Tough, old Top SGT shot in the throat right in front of him. Having to fire his rifle to release its bayonet from a Jap's belly. And after the guards opened fire on his patrol, how were they to know it was a Japanese field hospital and not an infantry unit? Doctors, nurses and patients screaming, bleeding, dying. New Guinea had been pure hell for the Sunset Division. Nick's breath caught in his throat, but he kept running. Eyes tearing, he screamed into the misty forest. *I should have jumped on the grenade first, Jim!*

Back at the gymnasium, Nick showered, put on his uniform and walked to his 1940 Plymouth convertible, parked at the nearby officer's club. Cruising past the drill field on the way to the family housing area, Nick slowed down, then pulled over to the side. A tough drill sergeant, with the look of a combat veteran, was training recruits. They looked pretty sharp and precise. Maybe they'd be ready for the next war— wherever it will be.

Nick glanced at the gasoline gauge. Damn! Almost empty. Better stop at Texaco on the way home. He lit a Lucky Strike with his battle-worn, Sunset Division Zippo and punched the first button on the Silvertone dashboard radio. Bing Crosby's rich, mellow baritone filtered through the smoky air like honey on bread right out of the toaster.

I'm dreaming of a white Christmas
Just like the ones I used to know

Where the treetops glisten and children listen
To hear sleigh bells in the snow

The gas station attendant came to the pump wearing an army field jacket over his Texaco uniform and a red star on his cap. "What'll it be, sir?"

"Fill her up, would you? Should take maybe 15 gallons."

Nick killed the engine and snuffed out his cigarette. He didn't die in New Guinea. And certainly didn't want to blow up while his gas tank was being filled. He chuckled ruefully to himself. Once a combat soldier, always on alert. Ease up, buddy. Sometimes it's best to just let things happen.

In the dim light of the Texaco station, raindrops pattered against the windshield, launching iridescent beads that streamed down in a race toward the cowl. Nick sat in the semi-darkness as the gas pump's flowmeter clicked rhythmically along. Five gallons. Ten gallons...

No moon as Jim and I slog through the ankle-deep mud in the rain forest. The point man's hand thrusts high in the air. We freeze. I scan the heavy green vines and trees all around us. Tap tap tap. What's that noise?

When the Texaco attendant tapped on the window, Nick snapped out of the flashback and rolled down the panel. "What do I owe you?"

"Took about fourteen gallons. $3.10."

Nick handed him four singles. "Keep the change, buddy. It's Christmas time."

The attendant took off his hat and beamed. "Thank you, sir! Merry Christmas."

Nick drove on to the family housing area at the north end of the post. Whenever his foot could be off the clutch pedal, he stretched his left leg to reduce the mild pain he'd learned to live with. Overall, things weren't so bad. It was Christmas time and he was off duty for the weekend.

Except for the nightmares and flashbacks, Nick was beginning to feel good again. He had a wife who really loved him. And his night time chemistry and engineering classes at the college were stimulating. For the first time in his life, he was actually enjoying school.

On active duty again, Nick stuck to his rigorous physical regimen like a Spartan warrior as he awaited assignment to occupied Japan. Fortunately, his temporary job at the Demobilization Center wasn't very demanding. He was usually in the Fort Lewis gym by 1700. Toss a medicine ball around, pull some weights, play a game of pickup basketball, then run four miles around the perimeter of the fort, rain or shine. Twice a week he took *Kempo* martial arts lessons from a private Hawaiian instructor.

Nick quietly opened the door of their two-bedroom bungalow and gazed into the kitchen at Ruth who was stirring a pot of baked beans on their Hotpoint stove. Wearing a tan apron over her woolen suit with padded shoulders and A-line skirt, his wife looked quite classy.

Turning toward the Frigidaire, Ruth started "Oh! I didn't hear you come in, sugar. How was your day at the center?"

Nick placed an arm around her waist and kissed her on the lips. "You know. Just a bunch of paperwork. Figuring out who has service scores high enough for demobilization." He opened a cabinet and grabbed a bottle of Old Grandad. "Can I fix you something, baby?"

"Rum and coke would be nice."

Ruth took a tomato and a block of Kraft cheese from the refrigerator. "I thought we could have toasted cheese sandwiches and beans tonight. I'm really tired. I taught two undergrad classes and a senior seminar today. Think we could just skip the movie tonight?"

Nick put ice cubes in two cocktail glasses and poured a shot of rum and Coca Cola in one, bourbon in the other. He handed Ruth her glass and clinked his against it. "We don't have to go out tonight, baby."

"Thanks. I really could use an early bedtime."

Ruth opened the bread box and selected four slices of Wonder bread. "It's great now that they've started slicing it again," she said, placing the bread in the toaster. "Let's just eat at the kitchen table tonight, if you don't mind."

After dinner, with Ruth leaning back on the sofa, Nick removed her Oxford shoes and gently massaged her feet. "What are you thinking about our assignment to Japan, baby?"

"I'm actually excited about it," Ruth said. "It'll be a great opportunity to practice what I've been teaching. The seminar I had with the seniors today was all about the Dewey theory. You know, teaching students how to think rather than rely on rote memorization. It will be pretty important for my job in Japan, I'd imagine."

Nick was proud that Ruth had used her academic connections to find a government job in the US Civil Information and Education (CIE) Section in Hokkaido. She was hard-working and ambitious. Unlike Nick who still harbored animosity toward all Japanese citizens, Ruth was more forgiving. Her sister had been killed in a terrible war. Almost by accident, she reasoned. Ordinary Japanese civilians had suffered greatly as well. She was ready to help them pick up the pieces of their shattered educational system. She'd even begun to learn conversational Japanese.

When Nick first learned that Ruth couldn't conceive children because of a ruptured appendix in childhood, he'd paused. He always assumed he'd have children. But soon, he realized how much he loved Ruth and felt resolved with the situation. He also knew that a military career with many prolonged absences could prove difficult for a conventional family. So Ruth without kids was really OK. And she wanted to pursue her own career.

Ruth moved closer to Nick on the sofa and ran her fingers through his hair. "What about you, sugar? Transportation isn't exactly your line of work as a combat officer. Is it? Think Hokkaido will be boring?"

"Not really. Rebuilding a rail system is intriguing for an engineering student." Nick paused, wrinkled his forehead and exhaled slowly. "What worries me is working with an enemy that almost killed me."

Ruth held his cheeks between her hands and looked directly into his eyes. "You're a pretty good, detail person. I know you'll study like a demon to learn about transportation systems." She shrugged. "As for the Japanese, you'll just have to keep a cool head." She wrapped her fingers around his wrist. "Don't worry. I'll help you."

In the semi-darkness of the streetlight, Nick sat naked on the edge of the bed waiting for Ruth to come out of the bathroom. When she opened the door, the dim street light silhouetted her lithe body through her chiffon nightgown.

Ruth walked barefoot across the room, allowing her nightgown to fall to the floor.

Nick drew her to him and buried his face in her belly. Ruth pushed him back onto the bed and laid down beside him, languidly tracing her fingertips along the deep scars that ran across his thigh. Stroking higher and higher, she whispered in his ear. "You're my soulmate and I'll never let you go."

They made ecstatic love. Rising and falling. Deeper and deeper until Nick felt he was dissolving into Ruth's body. Synchronizing himself with her rhythm, he held back as best he could until Ruth released a sigh of satisfaction and lay back on the sheets. Nick pulled the covers over them and gazed at Ruth's face in the faint light. How happy he was to be married to such a woman. After a year of great loss they seemed back on track.

A single, silvery tear glistened on Ruth's cheek in the darkness. Nick pulled her close. "What's wrong, baby?"

"Same old thing," Ruth said with a sniff of her nose. "How Emma and I were as kids together. Me the baby sister. That's where I learned about everything. Even sex. You and I were in perfect rhythm tonight. So I feel happy. But I also feel so very sad." Tears rolled down her cheeks. "My big sister is gone."

Nick knew there was nothing helpful to say, so he held her close and remained silent. Soon they both fell asleep. Nick slept until 0400 when he awoke into a familiar, distressing dream.

What's that scraping sound? A land crab? That's not the password! Something metal skips across the limestone. Then the flash. Jim doesn't hesitate a second. He jumps on the grenade first. Jim's gone and I'm blown sky-high.

"Wake up, sugar," Ruth said gently as she placed a cool hand on Nick's sweaty forehead. "Just another bad dream. You're OK."

1948

Chapter Twelve
SCAP

TOKYO—*While Americans are discussing the idea of reinforcing the United States position in Asia in view of a possible communist triumph in the Chinese Civil War, the British Commonwealth is quietly ending its share of the Japanese occupation...*

> New York Times
> December 15, 1948

Tokyo Japan
December 21, 1948

At 0800 Nick's footsteps echoed down the dark and musty hallway leading to the communications center in the basement of the Dai Ichi Building, headquarters of General Douglas MacArthur, the Supreme Commander of Allied Powers (SCAP).

Ribbons of electric-blue light flashed across the ceiling each time the radio operators, sequestered in cubicles on each side of the corridor, pressed their Morse code keys, firing up the vacuum tubes of their immense Signal Corps transmitters.

At the end of the hallway, light beaming through the glass panes of double doors spilled onto the concrete floor like wax melting from a saffron candle.

"Morning, sir," a sentry with a rifle slung across his shoulder said with a brisk salute. Nick returned the salute and stepped into the large, open room of the Com Center where rows of servicemen bent over their typewriters and clerks with clipboards of incoming data buzzed about like hummingbirds.

Nick rapped on the open office door of his superior officer Captain Robertson and saluted. "Got a minute, sir? I want to run something by you."

CPT Robertson, probably no older than Nick, looked up from his desk, piled with stacks of documents, gave Nick a half smile and gestured toward an empty chair. "Sure, Jackson. What's on your mind?"

"It's about the reports on Chinese troop deployments in Manchuria, sir. The numbers just don't add up."

CPT Robertson leaned forward. "What do you mean?"

Nick shifted his weight in the chair. "I read General Willoughby's most recent report to SCAP, sir." He hesitated. "The numbers seem to be significantly reduced from the incoming data I processed."

"In line with SCAP's estimates?"

Nick nodded.

CPT Robertson rose, shut the door, and sat back down. "Listen, Nick. Let me give you some advice." He paused for emphasis. "Don't go down this path. These are powerful guys. Way up high." He leaned forward. "Let it go. You're a seasoned combat officer, not a paper pusher. And who knows?

You may get your chance to fight again." He shook his head. "But if you go to war with the Baron over this, you'll lose everything."

Nick remained silent for a few moments. "Yeah. Maybe you're right, sir. It was just the principle that got me. I mean I saw the raw data come in."

CPT Robertson smiled like a benevolent mentor. "Look, Nick. Why don't you finish up early this afternoon and take a long run? Might clear your mind." He stood erect. "That's an order, Lieutenant."

At 1500, dressed in his running sweats, Nick nodded at the sentry as he exited the Dai Ichi building through a glass doorway, framed with elegantly shaped wrought iron panels. Heading north on Hibaya-dori Avenue, he began a counter-clockwise 3-mile run around the moat circling the gardens of the Imperial Palace.

Setting a brisk nine-minute per mile pace, Nick wove his way through the Japanese pedestrians strolling on the path around the water. Bundled up against the 40 degree chill, some wore traditional Japanese clothing, while others preferred the popular, western style. Few made eye contact as Nick bobbed and weaved along his route, intent to finish under half an hour.

Nick turned his face to take in the late afternoon sun. It was such a beautiful winter day to run his usual route. Even though bombs fell all around it during the war, the imperial palace and its grounds had been spared from Allied air attacks. Swans swam in the circular moat that was surrounded by walls and crisscrossed by bridges of chiseled stone. The park within was lush and green with knotty black pines, stands of bamboo and several temples with sculpted hedges, exotic statues and esoteric engravings. The imperial palace sat high in the middle of the gardens; though not as high as General MacArthur's sixth floor office in the Dai Ichi building.

After her remarkable success in Hokkaido, Ruth had been recruited to Tokyo a year ago by the Allied Command Civil Information and Education Section (CI&E). Her new job, helping the Japanese Ministry of Education develop a new public school curriculum was an exciting opportunity for an academic education specialist. Control of Imperial Japanese schools had been highly centralized. Rote memorization of textbooks without much pupil-teacher interaction was standard practice and creative thinking by students had been actively discouraged. Ruth, accompanied by Fumiko Suzuki, her Japanese teacher colleague from Hokkaido, worked each day in the Ministry of Education, a short walk from Nick's office in the Dai Ichi building.

Nick assumed his transfer to G2, the military intelligence section of SCAP in Tokyo, was meant to facilitate Ruth's acceptance of the CI&E offer. Although (as he often joked) it meant he ended up in the basement of the Dai Ichi building, he was very proud of Ruth. And, as it turned out, his work with G2 was quite interesting. Collating incoming information and updating military intelligence reports regarding the USSR, Communist China and North Korea, Nick felt he had a finger on the pulse of the region. But documenting military activity was one thing; being in actual combat another. Despite all the trauma and loss he'd experienced in the Pacific War, Nick remained a diehard infantry officer. And now he was ready for action again.

How things had changed over the two years he and Ruth had been in occupied Japan. In early 1946 destruction was everywhere, and hungry people roamed the streets in rags. Now the renewal of infrastructure was booming, and most Japanese seemed well-nourished, adequately dressed and healthy.

Although he was always treated with respect by Japanese citizens, Nick often wondered if the embers of animosity between old enemies were still glowing. He knew that he hadn't fully dealt with his own grievous attitude about Japan. It wasn't only the loss of Jim, his best friend ever. It was the whole New Guinea campaign. Just a brutal bloodbath—on both sides. Nick certainly killed quite a few Japs, but what they had done to some of his comrades in the 41st Battalion, he could never forget. But he was trying to let bitter memories go and relate to the Japanese people as ordinary human beings.

Herro baby! Came the familiar, friendly calls of the kimono-clad prostitutes lurking in the shadows and the Hollywood-style, *pan pan* girls leaning against the lampposts. Nick smiled as they waved him on by. They were bold, but he knew their lives were rough. His heart went out to them. *It always the women who take the war out of men.*

Suddenly, a large white bird burst from the moat beside him, beating its wings fiercely as it skimmed across the surface of the water.

Nick was back in the jungle. Japs and swamps all around.

Hyper alert, he ran faster.

Although startled at first, Nick quickly relaxed. It was just a swan. Soon he was back in rhythm, finishing the imperial course under 30 minutes. After a quick shower at the gym, he walked to the motor pool for a jeep ride to the officers' housing area in Yoyogi Park, about five miles west of the imperial palace. He'd be home by 1800, in plenty of time to help Ruth get ready for their dinner guests.

The route home took Nick through the Yamanote district of Tokyo. West of the Imperial palace, the district had been spared from Allied bombing until late in the war. The devastating firebombing of Tokyo in March 1945 focused on the docks, commercial areas and low-income neighborhoods east of the Imperial Palace.

In May 1945, however, the focus of attack shifted west to the prosperous Yamanote district. The Omotesando, a splendid tree-lined avenue famous for its fashionable boutiques and popular restaurants, was burned to the ground along with 3,200 people. Now repopulated with young, vase-shaped zelkova trees, their upright branches barren in midwinter, the Omotesando was the avenue that led to Nick's house in Yoyogi Park.

A light breeze stirred the branches of the young pines and barren maple trees interspersed with snags and charred trunks in Yoyogi Park as the driver dropped Nick off at the picket fence in front of his two-bedroom cottage in the Washington Heights Officer Housing complex. Amber light, filtering through the multi-paned windows of the kitchen and living room illuminated the gravel path leading to his front door. Good. Ruth was already home.

Ruth looked up from centering an embroidered Japanese table runner across the dining table and gave Nick a quick kiss and smile. "Hi, sugar. How'd it go today?"

"Not bad. I talked to Robertson about Willoughby's report. He said to let it go."

"Hmm." Ruth wrinkled her forehead. "Think he's right?"

"Not sure. But he is right about the risk of raising the issue. Particularly for someone at the bottom of the totem pole."

"Well. Maybe so."

"So how'd your meeting go?"

"The Japanese Education Ministry folks are dragging their feet a bit. But they'll come along. And Fumiko's been great. She really gets it."

Nick hung up his coat and kicked off his shoes. "Tell me about the new neighbors coming for dinner tonight."

"They just moved into the Heights last month. I met the wife at a Tupperware party last week. She's Cuban and he's Spanish-American from Texas."

Nick smiled. "Guess we'd better dig out our Xavier Cugat records. Is he army?"

"No. Air Force major. On Liaison with SCAP, I think. Better get changed now. They'll be here at seven."

When Nick opened the door at 1900, he was pleasantly surprised by the darkly, handsome couple standing before him. The man, dressed in a military overcoat open to a woolen sports jacket and striped necktie, held a woven straw basket with bottles of rum and soda, sprigs of mint and several limes. The woman, bundled up in a heavy winter coat, carried a covered dish with both hands.

"Ramón Morales," the man said, shaking Nick's hand.

The woman smiled. "I'm his wife Concepción."

"Please come in. I'm Ruth's husband Nick."

"Hello." Ruth emerged from the bedroom in a Kelly green dress with subtly squared shoulder pads, a narrow waist and pleated skirt that broke just below her knees. Nick thought she looked luscious.

When introduced to Ramón, Ruth's smile was warm and welcoming. Then she took the covered dish from Concepción as Nick helped her off with her coat.

An attractive, slender woman, Concepción wore a black wool dress with light gray Zebra stripes across the torso and shoulder pads more pronounced than Ruth's. "I've brought empanadas for, how do you say? Aperitivo?"

"Hors d'oeuvres," Ruth said softly. "Should we warm them?"

"We can eat them either way," Concepción said. "But these have beef picadillo in them. Better warm I think."

"Do you both like rum?" Ramón asked. Ruth and Nick shook their heads yes. "Then can I borrow your kitchen to make mojitos?"

With a tray of warm empanadas on the coffee table and mojitos in their hands, the two couples settled into the living room sofa and stuffed chairs. Nick put Frank Sinatra's new Christmas album on his RCA Victrola and turned the volume down low. "Where were you folks last stationed?" He asked.

"Hawaii," Ramón said.

"Nice place," Nick said. "Well, welcome to Japan."

"*Bienvenidos,*" Ruth said in her most graceful Spanish.

Concepción beamed. "*Gracias, Señora.*"

Just as Ruth predicted from her brief encounter at the Tupperware party, Concepción was a charming woman. With two children (watched by a baby-sitter tonight) she was a busy homemaker pleased to have a night out. Soon, the two women were in aprons preparing the meal in the kitchen.

Dinner was American style beef stew, Golden Goddess salad and Parker House rolls with twisted Christmas tree bread for dessert. Except for a little too much garlic in the stew and perhaps not enough Worcestershire in the salad dressing, Nick thought Ruth did a pretty good job. She sure cooked a helluva lot better than he ever could. Everyone seemed satisfied.

"What's it like in Cuba?" Ruth asked Concepción.

"I haven't been to Cuba for quite a while," Concepción said. "But I think it is calmer and more relaxed than here." She laughed. "Well, certainly more than here in Japan. I meant in the States."

"How are getting along with the Japanese?" Ruth asked.

"They seem a bit formal to me. But to be honest, with a couple of kids, I have little time to meet Japanese people living on the economy."

"I find them very interesting once you get to know them and maybe learn a little of their language," Ruth said. "I work closely with a Japanese teacher who is both my interpreter and friend. Like me, she lost family in the war. We actually have a lot in common. Maybe I could introduce you someday."

After dinner the women chatted in the kitchen as they did the dishes and the men stepped outside to smoke Havana cigars brought by Ramón.

"I heard it was your left leg," Ramón said. "Just like mine."

"Yeah." Nick patted his leg. "Hand grenade. You?"

"Shot down by a U-boat in the Caribbean. Can you believe that?"

Nick laughed. "Not a risk I've ever had in mind." He pointed to Ramon's leg. "Looks like you've healed pretty well."

"Just enough to pass the physicals to keep on flying. What about you? I hear you're a marathon runner."

"Well, some say I'm overcompensating, but the reality is I'm just trying to keep up my combat fitness skills."

"Where were you during the war?" Ramón asked.

"Mostly New Guinea." Nick swallowed a dark memory. "A real hell hole for us."

"After my shootout with the U-boat in '42, I saw action in the Philippines in '44," Ramón said.

"What were you flying?" Nick asked.

"During the war I flew a B-25. Now I'm in an B-26 Invader."

"They about the same?"

"No. B-26 is hotter. But once you know her, she flies pretty well."

"What was your mission in the war?"

"Mostly low-level ground support, some area bombing."

"So, what about now?"

"Hard to know from my lowly, liaison position in the Shogun's empire."

Nick laughed. He liked Ramón. The guy was funny in a sincere sort of way. "But basically your job is air support for ground forces, right?"

"Right."

"Oh man," Nick said. "Do I know about that."

"Believe me," Ramón said. "In the Pacific, we sure as hell tried to support you guys. Low-level strafing, napalm."

"Listen, buddy. You flyboys were manna from heaven for us grunts on the ground. I hope we never have to go through that again."

After their guests had gone, Nick turned to Ruth. "You go on up, baby, I'll finish the dishes left in kitchen and turn off the lights." Ruth gave him a peck on the cheek, and headed upstairs.

When Nick came into the dimly lit bedroom, Ruth was lying on their bed, eyes closed, smooth hips rounded beneath the covers. Nick stripped off his clothes and climbed into bed. But it was too late. Ruth was already snoring. So he snuggled up against her naked body and slowly drifted off to sleep.

Ruth was Nick's dream girl. Smart and beautiful. What more could he ask for in this life?

Chapter Thirteen
Hearts on fire

PYONGYANG, DPRK—*Become the sparks setting fire to the hearts of the masses and detonators giving full play to their mental power!*

> Slogan published in the 1948 Rodong Sinmun
> Central Committee Workers' Party of Korea

Pyongyang, DPRK
December 21, 1948

Snowflakes fell like glistening stars onto Ho-jun's black wool overcoat, then dissipated quickly as he picked up his pace through the streets around the Pyongyang Medical University Hospital. After an early morning departmental staff meeting and consultation with health care workers from neighboring Kangwon Province, he had just enough time for a brisk walk along the Taedong River before his public health lecture to the second year medical students.

The past two years had been the most stimulating of Ho-jun's career. In 1946 Choe Ung-sok, a renowned public health expert frustrated with the South Korean laissez-faire approach to healthcare systems, defected to the DPRK. When Choe became Dean of the Pyongyang Medical University, Ho-jun was able to obtain a two-year position as Choe's teaching assistant in the Department of Public Health and Hygiene. Now, a staff physician at the Pyongyang Medical University, he pursued a busy schedule of teaching medical students, collating epidemiological research data and developing public health strategies for the newly formed DPRK.

Ho-jun enjoyed these afternoon walks from the dour, four-story concrete hospital, built during the Japanese colonial period, to the elegantly arched 16th century Taedong Gate along the river. Under a slate-gray sky with lightly falling snow, he passed modern, Japanese-style buildings, older homes in poor repair, small shops and street vendors.

Crossing over the immense Kim Il-sung Square, Ho-jun maneuvered along a path swept clear of snow by municipal workers with straw brooms who scurried ahead of pedestrians like players at a curling match. At his destination, a two-story pavilion that was once the eastern gate of the ancient, walled city, Ho-jun paused to smoke a cigarette. Snow glistening in the graceful, curved rooftop arches of the ancient gate contrasted sharply with the dark granite of the building's walls. As Ho-jun watched his cigarette smoke swirl away in the brisk winter air, a warm feeling arose in his chest. He was proud of his Korean heritage.

On the way back to the hospital, Ho-jun stopped at a small restaurant for an order of *tteokbakki*, cylindrical rice cakes stir-fried with fish and sweet chili sauce. Fortified with a cup of corn silk tea, he was ready to return to work. The snowfall was heavier now, blanketing vehicles parked along the streets and muffling the usual sounds of the city at mid-day.

"Good afternoon, Comrade Doctor," the guard at the hospital entrance said with a brisk bow as Ho-jun headed back to his office.

At 1400 the medical students in their white coats, layered in rows above the lectern like seagulls on an ocean cliff, opened their notebooks in the cold, winter light streaming through the high-arched windows of the auditorium.

Ho-jun stepped up to the dark, slate board and wrote with slender chalk strokes:

Malaria control has three principal components:

1. Reduction of contact between vector and human host

2. Prevention of disease with prophylactic antimalarial drugs

3. Treatment of all episodes to minimize risk of transmission

"No single strategy can control malaria." Ho-jun paused to look into the attentive faces of the young students—mostly men, but also several women, chosen to reflect the ideal communist society. "Only the combined use of several partially effective methods can lead to adequate control of this endemic disease. Our government is strongly committed to administering the programs that are key to success in malaria control."

In the evening Alexei and his comely, blonde wife Olga, a Soviet education consultant fluent in Korean, picked Ho-jun up in their two-door GAZ coupe. Accompanying them in the backseat was Lee Min-ji, a young middle school teacher with satiny black hair and a pleasant smile. Olga had invited Min-ji to accompany Ho-jun at the preview screening of *My Home Village,* the state-run Korean Film Studio's first motion picture.

Only a few kilometers north of the city, the film studio was a maze of administrative and production buildings, revolutionary wall murals and neighborhood sets that vividly reproduced street scenes from China, Japan and Korea.

As usual at political events, Ho-jun, Alexei and their guests were assigned seats several rows back from the stage and had little interaction with the dignitaries present. But they enjoyed the film and looked forward to discussing it in the privacy of Ho-jun's downtown apartment in the Chung-guyok neighborhood.

It was a quiet weekday night on Sosong Street as they ascended the stairs to Ho-jun's third-floor apartment in a venerable, old building opposite the graceful Kimmy Boi Park.

"Please excuse the cold," Ho-jun said as he opened the heavy oak door. "We've had leaks in the central heating pipes. I'll burn some charcoal in the fireplace."

Arranged around a low table on the apartment's gleaming hardwood floor were thick, green mats woven from straw and hemp, a stuffed armchair and a sofa draped with lace. On the walls hung reproductions of an ancient Korean landscape and a 19th century impressionist painting of Paris in the rain.

Ho-jun took their coats and settled his guests in their seats of choice. Alexei and Olga sat on the couch. Ho-jun and Min-ji chose mats on the floor. After igniting some coal in an old, stone fireplace bordered with intricate ceramic designs, Ho-jun lifted the brass latch of an antique Chinese cabinet and turned to his guests. "Soju, sake or vodka?"

Alexei quaffed a shot of soju. "A lot like vodka. Clear, natural taste without the burn."

"Soju contains less alcohol," Ho-jun said.

"And it's not quite as sweet as sake," Min-ji added.

The conversation ranged from light to bittersweet. How were Ho-jun's monthly Korean People's Army reserve meetings? Was it difficult instituting a new curriculum in the public schools? How did Alexei and Olga feel about returning to Russia now that their liaison jobs were complete? What was Moscow like in the winter?

After a few rounds of potent alcohol, the conversation loosened up like a tight, new shoe once it's broken in. Feeling safe with one another, they began to express thoughts that would be dangerous to say in public.

"What did you think about the film?" Olga asked, her ivory skin reflecting the flickering light of flames from the fireplace.

Ho-jun smiled at Alexei. "Well…"

Alexei interrupted. "It was interesting to learn about Kim Il-sung's heroic leadership of the Korean People's Revolutionary Army."

Ho-jun chuckled. "Of course, the Chinese and Russians helped a little."

Alexei's face turned somber. "Have you read the latest *Rodong Sinmun*? Now Kim wants to be called "Great Leader.""

Min-ji sighed. "I'm worried we're becoming a police state. Just like under Japan. Remember the neighborhood watchdog committees? Media censorship? Now even our music has to be ideologically correct."

"I don't know," Alexei said. "Sometimes strict control by the government is necessary to maintain order. Particularly during the birth of a nation such as yours."

Ho-jun cocked his head. "Are you recommending concentration camps like Mao or Stalin?"

"No,"Alexei said. "But I don't think a true *Great Leader* should glorify himself and imprison his opposition. Nevertheless, clamping down on those that threaten the state may be necessary at times."

Olga leaned against Alexei's muscular shoulder and spoke in a soft voice. "Alexei and I know about repression. We lived through some bad times in the late '30s. Some called it *The Terror.* A lot of good people were liquidated."

"It's always the same," Min-ji said. "Power seeks growth and control. The Japanese tried to turn us into second class images of themselves. My father resisted and paid the price."

Ho-jun turned toward Min-ji with a raised eyebrow.

"He never came home from prison," Min-ji said.

There was a prolonged silence. Midst the safety of intimate friends, they'd spoken their minds. But they probably wouldn't do anything about it. Just be cautious, do their jobs and treasure moments of clear consciousness like this.

As Ho-jun leaned closer to Min-ji, the light falling across her high cheekbones stopped him for a moment. This was a beautiful and intriguing Korean woman. "What are you teaching now in the People's Middle School?" He managed to ask.

Min-ji locked her eyes with Ho-jun's for a deliciously long moment before speaking in a confident tone. "Under the Japanese, a third of our children didn't attend primary school and most adults were illiterate. Our new system is based on the Soviet model that Olga has been teaching me. It combines instruction in communist ideology with basic skills like literacy and mathematics. But our immediate goal is simple— get *every* Korean child in school."

Ho-jun smiled. He felt drawn to Min-ji like sand gliding across a beach in a heavy ocean wind.

1950

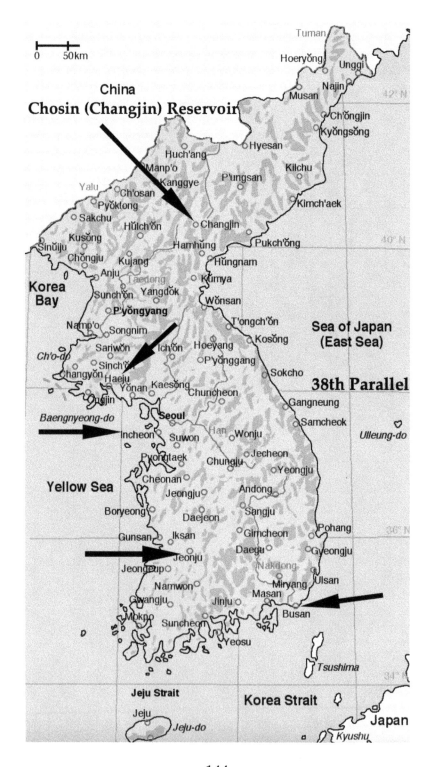

Chapter Fourteen
Crouching Amur

SEOUL, Korea—John Foster Dulles, special adviser to the Secretary of State, assured Korea today of continued United States support and predicted that the communists eventually would lose their grip on North Korea.

New York Times

June 19, 1950

Haeju, DPRK

June 24, 1950

At 0600, Ho-jun stepped outside of his 3rd Battalion officers tent into the humid, Saturday morning air. Although the Sixth Division of the North Korean People's Army (NKPA) had been on alert for several weeks in anticipation of a massive training exercise, Ho-jun had inveigled a day pass to meet his wife Min-ji in town. With a couple of kickstarts, his dark-green Russian *Dnepr* motorcycle roared to life and he was off to the Haeju railroad station.

Over the past few months, the North-South stand-off had heated up with each side threatening to attack the other. Recently, large numbers of NKPA troops and armor had been moved south toward the 38th parallel and civilians had been restricted from the border area.

Ho-jun hadn't seen Min-ji since March when his army reserve unit in Pyongyang had been activated and assigned to the newly formed NKPA 6th Division. Initially stationed at Sinuiju on the northwest border with China, the division was largely composed of former Chinese People's Liberation Army (PLA) personnel of Korean descent. Last month, the Sixth Division, was moved south to Haeju near the 38th parallel. Ho-jun's duty was to provide medical care to the troops— much as he'd done with the NAJUA in Manchukuo and the Soviet 88th Rifle Brigade in Russia.

The *Dnepr*'s 80cc engine assumed a pleasant rhythmic beat as Ho-jun cruised past oxen loaded with firewood, bicyclists on the way to work in the city and open fields reeking of night soil. He longed to hold his wife in his arms. He could almost taste her. In synchrony with the thrumming engine, he began to hum his favorite folk tune—*Arirang*.

Min-ji's train from Pyongyang was on time. When she stepped down from the platform of the coach, Ho-jun hugged and kissed her so fiercely that a tiny drop of blood trickled from the corner of her lips. *It's nothing,* she said, dabbing it with a white handkerchief that slowly became dappled with rose-colored spots. Holding her tight against his chest, Ho-jun leaned back and swung her from side to side, her boot tips barely skimming the wooden platform. Passersby smiled or nodded with approval. It was nice to see a soldier meeting his beloved. War seemed close. Who knew what could happen at any moment?

With a canvas backpack and laced, leather boots, Min-ji was dressed for a day in the countryside. Her white peasant blouse, cotton summer jacket and baggy trousers gathered at the ankles made her look more like a country girl than the sophisticated city dweller she was. Min-ji's hair swept across Ho-jun's neck as she mounted the leather seat perched above the rear fender of his motorcycle and wrapped her arms around his waist.

The streets were beginning to fill with pedestrians, bicyclists and military vehicles as they roared out of the city past a colorful billboard of the *Great Leader* Kim Il-sung surrounded by an adoring crowd. Soon there were only open fields, women in white bending over in rice paddies, peasants carrying bundles of straw and an occasional small town or isolated farmhouse.

Half-way up the mountain road toward Suyangsan Falls, they stopped for a white-bearded man goading his herd of dusty sheep across the road. Ho-jun idled the engine out of gear and leaned back to kiss Min-ji. It was a beautiful, cloudless day and he was with the love of his life.

At the foot of the falls, they parked the motorcycle and clambered across the boulders to sit by the waterfall cascading 128 meters down the steep face of the mountain. Min-ji placed a hand on Ho-jun's cheek. "I'm worried about you," she said, tears welling in the corner of her eyes. "The newspapers say an attack by the South could happen any day."

"Don't worry," Ho-jun said, using the term for a beloved spouse as he rocked her back and forth. "I've been through this before. Besides, our medical unit will be far to the rear in any battle." He stood in the full sun. "Let's take a walk by the river."

Picking their way along the rocky banks of the meandering river, they were soon in a solitary place where the water eddied adjacent to a marsh filled with reeds and lotus flowers. Their arrival startled a pair of white-naped cranes who flapped across the water, the red patches around their eyes glistening in the sunlight like carnival masks.

With the toe of her boot, Min-ji nudged the leaf of a white lotus flower rising above the muddy water. "The Buddhists say the lotus symbolizes resurrection."

Ho-jun laughed. "Well, maybe not resurrection. But they *do* close their flowers at night and reopen them in the morning."

"I just want to wake up with you in the morning," Min-ji said. "Every morning."

Ho-jun squeezed her hand. "It's all right. We'll be back together soon."

Min-ji spoke in a low, husky voice. "Let's find a quiet place," she said, turning toward the dense forest.

Hidden from the riverbank in a grove of larch and pine trees, they lay down on a bed of dry needles, tenderly undressed each other and made passionate love.

Munching a spicy rice cake from Min-ji's pack, Ho-jun lay naked on his back in the late afternoon sun streaming through the canopy of trees. Wait! Something was rustling in the forest nearby. He squinted into the dense foliage. Nothing. Then he saw them. Blue-green eyes fixed on his momentarily, then disappeared as a large, reddish-yellow animal covered with dark spots darted away. "*U-wa!*" Ho-jun exclaimed. "That was an Amur leopard!"

Min-ji sat up. "In the daytime? I thought they only came out at night."

"Maybe we chose a spot near his den," Ho-jun said.

"What do you think it means?" Min-ji said. "Such a rare animal visiting us?"

"I'm not superstitious," Ho-jun said. "But my grandfather would say it was a *Dokkaebi* bringing us a message. They can have various physical appearances, you know. But they're always fearsome."

"What message is this Dokkaebi's bringing us?"

"At the end of hardship comes happiness," Ho-jun said, echoing an old Korean proverb.

On the motorcycle ride back into town they passed a crumbling, old house with mud walls and a rice-straw thatched roof. Min-ji leaned forward and spoke into Ho-jun's ear. "I wonder if some *gwisin* live there," she joked. Ho-jun laughed. Dying before completion of a necessary task, *gwisin* were spirits remaining on earth to finish their work before passing into the underworld. Ho-jun downshifted the motorcycle on a curve. What unfinished tasks did he have?

At 1800 the sun was a golden-red ball shimmering on the horizon when Min-ji's train to Pyongyang disappeared in the distance. Ho-jun's boot tips scuffed languidly across the pavement as he returned to his motorcycle and rode back to camp.

Alone in his dark tent, Ho-jun sat on the edge of his cot. It had been a wonderful day, but he wasn't sure when he would see Min-ji again. He ignited the gas field lantern, took a long pull from a half-full bottle of soju and opened his weathered, leather-bound notebook. Raw emotions welled up inside his

149

chest like bubbles trying to escape from a boiling pot, but the words wouldn't come. Soon he fell asleep.

At 0200 Sergeant Hak, a handsome young corpsman with an intense gaze, burst into Ho-jun's tent. "Wake up, Comrade Doctor! We're being mobilized."

Ho-jun shook the cobwebs from his head. "Training exercise?"

"No. We're launching an attack south."

Chapter Fifteen
Sleeping Eagle

TOKYO—*Lieut. General Walton H. Walker, commander of the United States Eighth Army, said today,"...The men who argue that communism and not democracy guarantees fair distribution of wealth...are shrewd international bandits seeking to enrich no one but themselves. Communism, like all other isms, means only one thing—absolutism—power for a few and slavery for everyone else."*

New York Times
June 10, 1950

Tokyo, Japan
June 24, 1950

Razor-sharp blades of tall Kunai grass etched tiny, red scratches across Nick's cheek as he squinted through the lingering red smoke of the M18 hand grenades into the dense stand of twisted mangroves. Higgins and Riccardi had gone down before they'd gotten halfway across the field. But Nick still couldn't pinpoint where the machine gun fire was coming from. Drenched in sweat, he cautiously advanced, his finger resting firmly on the trigger of his rifle. Then dat dat dat dat dat, the woodpecker sound of the Japanese machine gun. Nick jumped for cover.

"Wake up, sugar," Ruth's hand tugged gently on Nick's shoulder, now halfway off the bed. "You're OK. It's just another dream." Brilliant light streamed through the bedroom window as she threw open the shade. "Looks like a nice day after all that rain. Should be fine for the picnic today."

At 1400 the temperature was 85 degrees F with 83% relative humidity in Yoyogi Park adjacent to the Washington Heights housing area. Backing away from the smoke streaming from the charcoal grill, Nick wiped sweat from his forehead with the back of his hand. He glanced around at the mixed crowd of Americans and Japanese from Ruth's job. Good. No one seemed to notice. He was still unsure about certain rules of Japanese etiquette. But wiping sweat from one's brow was probably considered rude. He leaned in toward the charcoal grill, waved the smoke away with one hand and resumed flipping the burgers and rolling the hot dogs from side to side.

When Nick turned to arrange the buns on the wooden picnic table, Ruth planted a strong kiss on his cheek. "Thank you, sugar. For being so nice to *all* my colleagues," she said. "It means a lot to me." Ruth melted back into the crowd, silently mouthing "Thank you."

"Do you cook them until they're all brown, Lieutenant?" Asked a handsome middle-aged Japanese man in a crisp white shirt and pleated trousers.

"Ah. Murakami-san," Nick said. "I try to cook them just to the edge of getting charred. So yeah. Deep brown."

Nick was beginning to open up to Murakami. As the former railroad station master in Hakodate, he'd been under Nick's command during the US Army occupation. Now an administrator in the Japanese National Railway network, Murakami lived with his wife Fumiko and two-year-old son Tadashi in Tokyo. Working closely with occupation authorities over the past few years, he had honed his English to a high level.

After suffering great personal losses in the vicious Pacific War, Nick still had difficulty seeing any Japanese person in a positive light. Although Murakami had been an excellent station master in Hokkaido, their personal relationship had been formal and restrained. Unlike Ruth, who had mastered basic conversational Japanese, Nick's knowledge of the language was rudimentary. But since Murakami's wife Fumiko worked closely with Ruth, Nick and Murakami often brushed shoulders. Although not exactly friends, their relationship was cordial.

Murakami gestured across the wide athletic field, complete with baseball diamond and running track. "Did you know the first Japanese airplane flew from this field in 1910?"

"I hadn't heard that, but I know it was an Imperial Army parade ground," Nick said as he piled hamburgers and hot dogs on a large platter. A bitter taste arose in his mouth. *They were training to kill us here not long ago. And here I am cooking goddam hotdogs for them.*

A crow high up in the branches of a white pine tree cawed loudly as the American and Japanese CIE workers converged on the picnic table. Layered with bowls of jello and potato salad, corn on the cob, potato chips, rolls and condiments, it was the first time many of the Japanese employees had tasted real American picnic food. On a side table lay chocolate and pineapple upside down cakes, chocolate chip cookies, brownies and an ice chest filled with Coca Cola, 7-up and Dr. Pepper.

Nick and Ruth sat with Murakami, Fumiko and their two-year-old son Tadashi on a plaid woolen blanket spread across the grass. Fumiko fed Tadashi a bite of mashed up hamburger and settled him down to play with a set of *Tumi Ishi* wooden blocks.

Murakami took a sip of Dr. Pepper and wrinkled his nose. "Tastes a bit odd, don't you think?"

Ruth laughed. "They say you either love it or hate it. I'll stick with 7-Up."

"What are you working on now," Nick asked Fumiko.

"Mostly textbooks," Fumiko said in excellent English, albeit with pronunciation that was a bit less polished than her husband's. "We're creating some exercises that promote problem solving skills."

"It's quite a change from the old system," Murakami said. "I don't recall a teacher ever asking me what I thought. It was all about memorization."

"With the new curriculum, teachers actually help children evaluate and solve social problems," Ruth said.

"How do they do that?" Nick asked.

"With young children, the teachers play games like *yubin-gokko*," Fumiko said.

Nick glanced at Ruth.

"*Yubin-gokko* means post office," Ruth said. "It mirrors problem solving in social situations. The older kids participate in *yamabiko-gakko* or echo school."

"That's where they write essays about their personal lives," Fumiko added.

"It sounds like an exciting time for educators," Nick said.

"Well, when everything falls apart, opportunity arises," Ruth said.

"How are things going with the railroad, Murakami-san," Nick asked.

"With assassinations and sabotage by the extreme left, it's been a difficult year, Lieutenant," Murakami said. "But it looks like things are calming down now and more moderate union members are speaking up. As we say in Japan: after a storm, things will stand on more solid ground."

"It's hard to know where the communist threat is going these days," Nick said. "After the May Day riot the police sure cracked down."

"Yes, but the government just rescinded the order banning political demonstrations," Ruth said.

"That was with pressure from MacArthur," Nick said. "He says he doesn't want to see a police state develop on his watch."

"Nevertheless, the police are still raiding communist newspaper offices, unions and student groups," Murakami said. "And yesterday a US military court sentenced four young communists to hard labor for their open letter to General MacArthur."

"Open letter?" Ruth asked.

"Challenging the crackdown on leftists," Nick said.

Tadashi flipped a wooden block into the potato salad on Ruth's paper plate. "*Mō yamete!*" Fumiko said, grabbing his wrist. You stop that now!

At 1800, with the temperature still 81 degrees F, Nick and Ramón sat in the shade of tall pines in Nick's backyard.

"How'd it go up at Johnson this week?" Nick asked, referring to the Air Force base about an hour and a half north of Tokyo.

"No problems. I got in my four hours of flight time in the B-26. It felt good to be in the air again. I'm not cut out for this desk job at SCAP."

Nick took a long pull on his Budweiser. "Me neither, pal. But I'm keeping up my combat skills. I run a few miles every day around the imperial palace. Take Kempo lessons. Try to get out on the firing range at least once a month."

"How long do you think we'll have to stay here?" Ramón asked. "Seems like occupation withdrawal is in the air. What are you hearing?"

"Well, don't hold your breath, Ray. These days MacArthur's talking about a coordinated defense plan for the entire Western Pacific."

"Guess that means we aren't leaving Japan soon."

"Probably not. Despite mixed messages from the State Department, it looks like the Formosa standoff is on the front burner."

"What about Korea?" Ramón said.

Nick raised an eyebrow. "Well, there has been a lot more noise along the 38th parallel recently."

"Saber rattling. Nothing new, right?"

"I guess not, but recent intel makes me a bit edgy." Nick said.

"What do you mean?"

"Increased North Korean troops and vehicles along the 38th."

"Any significance?"

"Not so sure, Ray. Willoughby's playing it down. But we're also seeing increased Chinese movement along the Manchurian border."

"The State Department thinks North Korea wouldn't make a move without Russian approval, right?"

"Yeah. And the Russkies are probably not up for another world war."

"Not just yet anyway."

Chapter Sixteen
Striking South

SEOUL, Korea—*Northern Pyongyang radio broadcast a declaration of war at 11 A.M. North Korean forces attacked generally along the border, but chiefly in the eastern and western areas, in heavy rain after mortar and artillery bombardments which started at 4 A.M.*

United Press
June 25, 1950

Crossing the 38th Parallel
June 25, 1950

Staccato bursts of rain swept across the windshield of the Russian ZIS-5V cargo truck, slathering a thin layer of gray-green mud across its chipped surface in the shape of a finely striated fan. The whine of the truck's transmission rose and fell as the driver, a grizzled veteran of the Manchurian campaign, shifted between third and fourth gear to keep aligned with the other four vehicles of the 3rd Battalion medical treatment squad.

Ho-jun's eyes remained fixed on the murky, dawn horizon that sporadically burst aflame with golden-red clusters of Katyusha rockets, mortar fire and field artillery explosions.

Focusing on the constant whir of the truck's tires over the wet pavement like a prayer wheel mantra, he tried to calm his mind. Breathing in stillness, breathing out tension—just as his father had taught him as a child. Only hours ago, Ho-jun lay in Min-ji's arms. Now he was off to war again and he knew what to expect.

The main force of the NKPA Sixth Division, in a convoy of troop carriers, tanks, mounted artillery, supply vehicles and munition trucks, had already swept south through Kaesong just before dawn. Ho-jun's squad of six medical corpsmen and five driver/aides now brought up the rear with three trucks carrying medical supplies and two ambulances for evacuation of the severely injured back to Pyongyang. In Kaesong, an ancient walled city surrounded by mountains, the team would set up a temporary aid station designed to perform triage and necessary urgent care before moving further south with the advancing North Korean forces.

Ho-jun glanced through the rear window into the truck bed where his 20-year-old chief corpsman SGT Hak, along with two other corpsmen, sat in the cool rain, wedged between stacks of medical supplies. Raindrops ricocheted off their helmets and cascaded through the folds of their ponchos like streams of silver beads. Ho-jun shifted his warm boots on the vibrating floorboard. At times it was nice to be an officer.

The grade steepened as they climbed into the *Ahobiryong* Mountain range and the odor of burning petroleum began to fill the air. The driver shifted down as they approached a cloud of jet-black particles tinged with crimson sparks that was spreading across the highway. A NKPA soldier with a light-weight Soviet submachine gun slung over his shoulder, waved his hands up and down in a gesture to decrease speed.

Creeping along with the plaintive whine of low gear, they passed an NKPA half-track with its anti-aircraft gun blown askew, rear treads unravelled and fire belching like a blowtorch from its steel-plated cabin. Three bodies covered with dark-green tarpaulins lay along the roadside. Ho-jun's driver briefly bowed his head. "Death doesn't erase good deeds, Comrades," he said, blending a Buddhist exhortation for the dead with his communist beliefs.

Several damaged NKPA and ROK vehicles lay abandoned along the highway on the ascent to the pass above Kaesong. At the top of the pass they pulled off the road behind a Russian-built T-34 tank for a brief rest. Five NKPA crewmen in leather helmets, leaning against their idling tank, snapped to attention as Ho-jun approached.

"*Anyoung haseyo!*" Good morning, Ho-jun called out with a brisk salute as he strode toward an outcrop of rock that offered a panoramic view of the medieval trade capitol of the Goryeo kingdom. Dark clouds of smoke spiraled skyward from multiple parts of the walled city that lay in a valley traversed by rolling hills and two small rivers. South of the city on the distant horizon silent bursts of orange light illuminating the dark underbellies of rain clouds were followed by a low rumbling sound. Ho-jun estimated the time delay between the flashes and sound—the active combat zone was probably about 15 kilometers south of Kaesong.

Pockmarked with random shell craters, the road into the northern sector of the city resembled a desolate, lunar landscape. Scorched vehicles and twisted military equipment lay along the wayside. The walls of some buildings remained standing while their roofs had been blown away. Groups of bewildered citizens covered with soot silently picked through smoldering piles of rubble, seeking anything familiar and intact. A bedraggled woman carrying an infant with a bandaged head stumbled aimlessly through the debris like a dreamer half-aroused from a nightmare. Ho-jun felt a burning sensation in the back of his throat. These were innocent victims of his army's onslaught.

Ho-jun's medical team commandeered an undamaged, Hanok-style home in an affluent neighborhood near the city center. With a main hall and several outbuildings covered with arched tile roofs arrayed around a large courtyard, it was an ideal setting for an aid station. The owner, an elderly man with a long, white beard and *jeogori* jacket over baggy white trousers, became agitated when the team demanded entrance to his home. He was soon calmed, however, by SGT Hak's assurance that no one would be harmed, his men would not enter the women's quarters and the team would be gone by dawn.

SGT Hak ordered three of the drivers to unload necessary medical equipment and set up an aid station in the men's hall of the compound. He and Ho-jun then set out in the ambulances to find the NKPA casualty clearing station that was usually placed near a transportation facility. Accosting a pedestrian, who trembled as if seeing *Bul-Gae*, legendary fire dogs from the dark world, they obtained directions to the railroad station.

Severely damaged by a battle in the early morning hours, the station's roof had collapsed, and the walls were riddled with bullet holes. On the pavement in front of the building, three 6th Division combat corpsmen were attending to thirty wounded soldiers lying on blood-stained blankets. Another dozen, their faces covered with tarpaulins, lay in a silent row along the sidewalk.

One of the corpsmen approached Ho-jun and saluted. "We're glad you're here, Comrade Doctor. These men were too severely injured to move on with their units. Once you take them, we'll try to catch up with our advance forces."

After Ho-jun and SGT Hak were briefed on each patient, they dismissed the corpsmen, divided the patients between themselves and performed a rapid three-level triage used since the Napoleonic wars: I=dangerously wounded, II=less dangerously wounded and III=slightly wounded.

The twenty soldiers in categories II and III were loaded, three at a time, into the ambulances and transported to the ad hoc aid station in the commandeered Hanok house. While the ambulance drivers made repeated trips to the aid station, Ho-jun and SGT Hak tried to make the ten soldiers doomed to category I as comfortable as possible. Some of these men were unconscious while others emitted low-pitched moans like wind sighing through the pines. A few lay alert and listless, their empty gaze turned toward the leaden sky.

Like tender parents at bedtime, Ho-jun and SGT Hak gently wrapped the dying men in blankets, injected each with two syrettes of morphine and left them at the railroad station. Neither Ho-jun nor SGT Hak spoke on the way back to the aid station.

In the men's hall of the commandeered home, the team had set up a treatment area with mats and blankets spread over the hardwood floor. Ho-jun and SGT Hak walked briskly around the room, receiving the corpsmen's assessment of each injured man. The condition of three patients was particularly critical—one with a chest wound and difficulty breathing, a delirious man with a head injury and another with a compound femoral fracture that required an external traction splint.

SGT Hak immediately took charge of the team, assigning treatment of the less severe injuries, such as minor bullet wounds, lacerations, closed fractures and burns, to the corpsmen and aides. Then he assisted Ho-jun with management of the most critical patients.

A soldier with a bullet wound to the chest, frothy red sputum and difficulty breathing had first priority. Ho-jun removed the chest bandage and made a quick assessment. "Good. The entry wound is lateral and above the nipple line— less risk of injury to abdominal organs." He listened to both lung fields with his stethoscope. "Breath sounds are asymmetrical. What's the first thing we need to think about, Sergeant?"

"Tension pneumothorax," SGT Hak said.

"Correct. Let's log roll him over and look at his back."

Noting the exit wound on the back was twice as large as that on the chest, Ho-jun spoke in a lowered voice. "There's probably significant lung damage. High risk for empyema later on."

SGT Hak opened the chest tube kit and laid out a large bore needle and syringe. Ho-jun swabbed the patient's upper chest wall with iodine and alcohol, then pulled on a pair of surgical gloves. "You want to go in the mid-clavicular line just above the second rib to avoid the blood vessels on the bottom edge," he said.

Ho-jun slid the needle over the rib until he felt a distinct pop, and a rush of air hissing through the needle. He then attached the needle to a syringe and aspirated the free air several times until the flow ceased. The patient took several deep breaths, then proceeded to breath normally. Ho-jun removed the needle and placed a petroleum jelly dressing tightly over the area. "Next time you do it, Sergeant," he said.

Ho-jun's medical team worked late into the night. He and SGT Hak successfully applied an external traction device to the compound fracture patient and stabilized the soldier with the bullet wound to the chest. Unfortunately, there was little they could do for the soldier with the head injury. He was dead before midnight.

June 26, 1950

After three hours of sleep, Ho-jun was back in the ZIS-5V truck heading south to catch up with the NKPA forces now advancing toward the port of Incheon. If all went well, his 3rd Battalion Treatment Squad would set up a field station just south of Gimpo, about 10 kilometers north of the Incheon battlefield.

Closing his eyes, Ho-jun began composing a love poem to Min-ji based on the rhythm of an ancient lament known to every Korean—*The Song of the Yellow Bird.*

When we startled the cranes
As we lay together in the forest
They all flew off so smoothly
Fly away with me

Chapter Seventeen
The Great Nakdong Offensive

TOKYO—In the United States 25th Division sector four enemy attacks were repulsed by elements of the division. These attacks were supported by heavy mortar barrages. Units of the division destroyed an enemy pocket in the rear of their positions killing forty Reds. Another unit repulsed an enemy attack after a brief fire fight.

New York Times
September 15, 1950

East of Jeonju, Republic of Korea
September 15, 1950

Ho-jun clamped the large vessel pulsating deep within the shrapnel wound on the soldier's leg and successfully ligated it with a heavy suture. Over his shoulder he spoke to SGT Hak. "Can you close this up? I'd better get to that head wound."

With his eyes stinging, Ho-jun inadvertently wiped beads of sweat from his forehead with his sterile glove, leaving a streak of blood across his eyebrow.

"Comrade Doctor, you...," said the female corpsman.

Ho-jun cut her off. "No time for sterile measures. We're running out of medical supplies." He held out his gloved hands. "Just rinse these off, please."

As the corpsman reached for a bottle of sterile water, a large fly that had been scavenging a pile of bloody bandages zipped to the top of the open tent and buzzed about, trapped in the warm, late morning sun. It seemed ironic. Only a few months ago Ho-jun's major concern had been control of infectious diseases spread by insect vectors in the North. While malaria, dysentery, typhoid fever and tuberculosis were still of major concern in the war zone, they were secondary issues now. The bloody fighting for control of the 600-meter-high ridge nicknamed "Battle Mountain" was keeping his 3rd Battalion medical treatment squad busy day and night.

Each morning UN forces blanketed the ridge with artillery and mortar fire. Their bombers strafed, blasted and dropped napalm on positions that had been seized overnight by the NKPA. Then American and ROK troops retook the ridge with bloody, hand-to-hand fighting that lasted until twilight. But in the middle of the night, after heavy artillery and mortar shelling of UN positions, the NKPA retook the summit.

This seesaw battle for the high ground overlooking the approach to Busan had been raging for several weeks, and control of the ridge had changed hands twenty times. Casualties on both sides were massive with no end in sight.

The NKPA 6th Division was replenishing its ranks with forcibly conscripted South Koreans. To assure participation by these reluctant warriors, rifleman bringing up the rear during an attack had orders to shoot any deserters. With no such shoot to kill policy, UN forces were plagued with "bug outs" mainly by ROK and rancorous American draftees.

Although an experienced veteran of many battles in Manchuria and South Korea, Ho-jun felt the battle for this mountain top seemed extremely vicious. Much of the combat involved hand-to-hand fighting, the same savage tactics employed by all warriors across time. There was a lot of ugly death on both sides. And recent reports that his own troops had executed UN POWs? *Dodaeche.* What the hell? What happened to the noble mission of reuniting the Korean people after years of subjugation?

Since the end of June the NKPA steamroller had advanced rapidly south. Now UN forces were aligned behind a semi-circular perimeter around the port of Busan with their backs to the Sea of Japan. Victory for the North Koreans appeared to be imminent. But UN resistance was stubborn and their reinforcements were on the way. Most important, NKPA casualties were mounting and supply lines from the North were dangerously overextended.

Ho-jun scanned the dozen cots filling the medical tent and the rows of wounded lying on stretchers in the sun. His squad of six medical corpsman and five ambulance driver/aides were busy tending to soldiers with bullet and mortar wounds. Napalm burns. Fractures and concussions. Close quarter bayonet lacerations.

A female corpsman led Ho-jun to the cot of a new admission with a severe head injury. "He was hit around midnight, Comrade Doctor. But the stretcher bearers ran into sniper fire on the way down the west side of the ridge. They didn't get here until a few minutes ago."

"Vital signs?"

"Blood pressure 160 over 80. Pulse 120. Respirations 8. Unconscious."

Ho-jun leaned over the soldier and cautiously removed the blood-soaked bandage from his left temple. A 10-centimeter, full thickness avulsion revealed no active bleeders. "What do you think?" He asked the young corpsman.

"Severe head injury with hypertension," the young woman replied.

"I agree. Not much we can do out here. With so many urgent cases, he'll be low priority for transportation to the rear. Let's just try to keep him comfortable."

"I do have a question, Comrade Doctor," the corpsman said. "If he *did* survive, what kind of brain damage might he have?"

"Left temporal lobe injury. What does that make you think of?"

The corpsman hesitated. "Memory?"

"Correct. But also language and right-sided movement." He turned toward the row of cots. "Let's move on."

At twilight, despite continued admissions and several deaths during the day, the team seemed to be catching up. SGT Hak approached Ho-jun and untied his face mask. "You should get some rest, Comrade Doctor. You've hardly slept since we captured Jeonju."

Ho-jun sighed. "What about you?"

"I've had a few hours here and there, Comrade Doctor. I'll get our corpsmen to cover you for a few hours."

Ho-jun stumbled into his small tent and collapsed on the cot. Unraveling the purple scarf wrapped around an elegantly carved bamboo picture frame, he gazed at the photograph he'd taken of Min-ji taken last winter. Wrapped in a fur coat in front of Pyongyang's famed Taedong Gate, she looked like a beautiful, *Goryeo* princess. With a sigh, Ho-jun relaxed his tense muscles. He imagined Min-ji dissolving the sorrow and hardship of his day. He could smell her. Taste her. Melt into her arms. He fell asleep in less than a minute.

A few hours later Ho-jun was awakened by SGT Hak. "Important news, Comrade Doctor. The Americans have landed at Incheon."

Like a diver emerging from the depths, Ho-jun was slow to clear his head of deep sleep. Then he grasped the situation. They were now trapped between an invading UN force from the north and the advancing defenders of Busan in the south. Supply routes would be cut off. Scant medical supplies would not be replenished. They had to retreat north as fast as possible to avoid entrapment by UN forces.

Chapter Eighteen
Crosscut

TOKYO—From a military strategy viewpoint, the United Nations invasion of North Korea today was a sound operation... General Douglas MacArthur hit the North Korean Communists with the same punch that made him famous in World War II and the landing at Inchon bore the general's trademark. Hit them where they are light and cut them off was General MacArthur's strategic creed when he fought the Japanese from New Guinea through the Philippines from 1942 to 1945.

New York Times
September 15, 1950

Seoul, Republic of Korea
September 25, 1950

After mastering the enormous tides, broad mud banks and towering sea walls at Incheon ten days earlier, the US Army 1st Battalion/32 Infantry Regiment (1/32 IN) was rolling along the right flank of the 1st Marines on the drive toward Seoul. Advancing through minefields and sporadic attacks by NKPA tanks and infantry, they now approached a deeply entrenched enemy arrayed in well-planned, defensive positions around the city. Control of the capital city held great significance for both sides, and the NKPA was putting up fierce resistance.

As they approached the western sector of Seoul, the 1st Marines encountered savage opposition and had been unable to break through into the city center. The 32nd Infantry Regiment and the 17th ROK Regiment were now tasked with clearing NKPA troops from three hills dominating the southern approach to the city. On Monday morning, after a sustained artillery barrage, the US 32nd and the 17th ROK began crossing the Han River.

At 0630 fog hovering over the water like a heavy, gray blanket was just beginning to lift, but Nick still couldn't see more than a few yards in front of the tracked, landing vehicle (LVT). Nicknamed *alligator* after its origin as a civilian rescue vehicle designed to operate in swampy areas, the amphibious LVT churned toward the northern bank of the river. Nick squinted into the fog. *Good.* There could be no effective NKPA fire until visibility improved. And hopefully, by that time his 4th Platoon would be advancing east through the trees along the southern bank of the Han River.

Nick stared aft into the exhaust fumes of the LVT engine billowing above the dark water like the murky expiration of a fire-breathing beast. He inhaled the blackened hydrocarbon particles and felt the thrum of the seven-cylinder engine reverberating beneath his feet. Nick knew this state of consciousness well. Before a battle he always became hyper-alert, tuned into all of his senses. He rolled his shoulders and stretched his neck trying to relieve the tension. Then he ran his fingertips down the smooth curve between the grip and stock of his semi-automatic M1 carbine as if it were the voluptuous contour of Ruth's lower back.

With half the weight and a less powerful cartridge than the standard M1 Garand carried by infantrymen, the carbine was issued to officers and support troops who were not expected to be fighting on the frontline. Nick preferred the range and accuracy of the Garand, but it was nice carrying the lighter carbine. It nestled smoothly against his shoulder and, at a distance, could outshoot the Russian Mosin-Nagant rifle and the rapid fire, close quarter PPSh-41 *burp gun* favored by the NKPA.

On board the LVT were sixteen men under Nick's command. The other half of his platoon would arrive on the next LVT crossing the Han. By mid-day, all battalions of the 32nd Infantry and the 17th ROK regiments would be on the north side of the river.

After the *alligator* nosed onto the northern bank and dropped its steel jaws, Nick's men slogged through a muddy stream that was up to their knees and waited for the rest of the platoon on higher ground. Nick gazed uphill through the gauzy fog which was beginning to burn off with the morning sun. A few scattered rifles crackled. Then sudden bursts of machine gun fire raked the lower slopes hurling clods of soil into the air.

Sergeant Mike Miller was the first to respond. "Hit the dirt!" he yelled as he scanned the slope for the source of fire.

Nick dropped down with Miller behind a fallen tree trunk. "Can you see them?"

Slowly scanning the slopes back and forth, Miller shook his head.

Then another burst of machine gun fire.

"There!" Nick pointed toward a stack of brush.

"Hell. It's only about 50 yards up slope," Miller said. He unfastened a grooved, Mk II hand grenade from his belt and pulled the pin. With Nick's rifle fire covering him, Miller rose and threw the grenade like a skilled, third baseman on a double play. The grenade exploded right on top of the machine gun nest.

"OK boys. Let's sweep those upper slopes," Nick said, advancing up the hill in a semi-crouch, scanning the terrain with his rifle. *Nothing.* All quiet. Then gunfire as six NKPA soldiers leapt from a hidden trench firing rifles and burp guns. Two of Nick's men were hit before all the firepower of his platoon took five of the enemy soldiers down. The remaining NKPA soldier ran but was picked off by a volley of shots before he could reach the forest on the edge of the hillside.

Nick slowly walked through his platoon, assessing the damage. Private Hawkins dead. Sanders required evacuation. A minor hand wound on Campanella. Everyone else pretty intact. Not a great trade off, but it could have been worse. And SGT Miller was outstanding. Although they honored the semi-formal relationship between platoon commander and First Sergeant, Nick really liked Miller. They had a lot in common. During the last war they both were enlisted men in the bloody New Guinea campaign. And both had been wounded. And since the men liked him, he got things done. Nick knew he could always rely on his right-hand man Mike Miller.

By late morning the 2,32 and 3,32 battalions were climbing high on the slopes south of Seoul. As a result, the NKPA small arms and machine gun fire was now directed further uphill, and Nick's men of 1/32 could concentrate on moving east to clear the area adjacent to the banks of the Han River. Except for a few sporadic firefights with hidden snipers, the 4th platoon saw little action.

In the early afternoon an M4 Sherman tank from the 32nd Regiment came lumbering along the shore like an irate rhinoceros with a platoon of 17th ROK infantrymen flanking either side. Nick saw that the tank, bristling with a .75 mm cannon and 50 caliber and .30 caliber machine guns, had one modification. In place of its second bow-mounted .30 caliber machine gun was the nozzle of a mechanized flame thrower.

"Now we've got a Zippo," Miller said. "Just like we had on New Guinea."

"Flame tanks got us through Biak," Nick said. "Well almost." *A vivid image flashed through his mind. A pineapple-shaped hand grenade skipping across the coral. Jim getting to it first...*

Nick spat on the ground, shaking off the memory as he approached the ROK officer in charge of the platoon.

"I'm LT Lee," the ROK officer said with a brisk salute.

Nick studied the ragged scar running across the ROK officer's cheek as he returned the salute. "Jackson. Glad you can join us." He gestured uphill. "Most of the action's up there. So far not too much down here."

"We cleared some hidden trenches since crossing the river at Yeongdeungpo," LT Lee said with a slight roll of the *r* in the word river. "Fire tank was big help."

Nick gave an emphatic head nod. "You guys can take the lead."

In the late afternoon one of the ROK scouts spotted some movement in the burgundy-colored leaves of a large viburnum shrub spreading between boulders on the hillside. Alerted by LT Lee, the Sherman tank turned uphill and rumbled toward the suspicious site.

As the tank's cannon swiveled toward its target, NKPA machine gun fire erupting through the leaves pinged harmlessly off the heavily armored turret in a shower of thin, red sparks.

Then, with a fiery bang and a puff of gray smoke, the tank's cannon obliterated the shrubs and boulders and exposed an opening to a smoky cave. When the smoke and dust cleared, several NKPA soldiers in blood-soaked, olive green uniforms lay at the cave entrance among fragmented sand bags and a scorched Soviet *Goryunov* SG-43 machine gun.

From deep within the shadows, a platoon-sized group of over 30 NKPA infantrymen began to charge out of the cave. Firing burp guns and rifles, the soldiers were met by a roaring, 20-foot flame that swelled at its tip into the shape of an oily rose, six feet in diameter. While most of the attackers were incinerated on the spot, one NKPA soldier ran downhill, completely aflame like a comet tumbling through the atmosphere. *Poor bastard,* Nick thought as he raised his rifle and killed the screaming man with a single shot. The remaining NKPA soldiers within the cave dropped their weapons and surrendered.

September 26, 1950

By mid-afternoon, after taking the three hills south of Seoul and fighting off several NKPA counter attacks, the US

32nd and ROK 17th regiments had cleared their zone of the enemy and established contact with the Marines on the eastern side of the city.

As the Marines proceeded into bloody, street-by-street fighting in the center of Seoul, the Army's 7th Division was ordered south where, after overcoming stiff resistance, they captured Suwon and Osan. On September 27 the 1st Cavalry Division, fresh from their breakout on the southern tip of the Korean peninsula, arrived at Osan and linked up with the troops from the Incheon landing. The US Army 7th Division then began a long overland truck march to the east coast port of Busan.

October 12, 1950
Busan, South Korea
At 1900 orange-red cumulus clouds were beginning to dissolve on the western horizon, while the undersides of clouds to the east were tinted indigo against the pale-blue sky. Women dressed in white, carrying bundles on their heads, mingled with Koreans in western dress and uniformed soldiers strolling along the waterfront lined with fishing boats and naval ships of all sizes.

Traffic was light as vendors on the docks began packing up the unsold remnants of the day's catch—a remarkable variety of fish, crustaceans, aquatic creatures and edible sea plants. Nick tuned in to the vibrant thrum of the crowd and the exotic mixture of salt air, petroleum fumes and creatures taken from the sea. A chilly sensation spread across his neck. How close this bustling seaport had come to being overrun by the relentless NKPA. But now the tide had turned, and the North Koreans were retreating back home.

Turning up an alley lined with crates, barrels and store fronts, he came to a street with scattered bars and a few restaurants.

"What's up, baby?" A young Korean woman in a slinky, silk dress purred from the shadows as Nick strolled by. He smiled at her but kept on walking until he came to the Lucky Starfish, a popular bar among Americans and Korean girls seeking a little excitement.

Several GIs were sitting at the bar, tossing down glasses of Soju with bottles of *Hite* beer as a chaser. A graceful Korean bar girl, balancing a tray of bottles and glasses on her arm, wove about the smoke-filled room like a lissome hummingbird at twilight. At a corner table, a boyish GI was engaged in an intimate conversation with a beautiful Korean girl dressed in orange satin. *Somewhere there's heaven. How high the moon*...Les Paul and Mary Ford crooned from a scratchy 78 spinning on a portable Zenith record player behind the bar.

Nick's boots thudded heavily over the ceramic tile floor as he passed between tables in the dimly lit room toward a luxurious potted palm bathed in pale yellow light. At a small table in the corner sat Ramón in his khaki USAF uniform, puffing on a cigarette and nursing a glass of imported Japanese Asahi beer. For the first time in days Nick felt comfortable and relaxed. It was great to see his old friend from Tokyo.

As soon as he saw Nick, Ramón leapt to his feet. Ignoring Nick's outstretched hand, he grasped Nick's shoulders. "Glad you're OK, man. I've heard what you've been through."

Nick was taken a little aback by the Latin intimacy of Ramon's gesture. In the Northwest, intense moments like seeing your friends emerge alive from battle, were met with a firm handshake and maybe grasping of the forearm with the other hand. But he was genuinely glad to see Ramón again. It reminded him of the happy home life he'd had with Ruth in Tokyo before this bloodbath had begun.

"Great to see you, Ray. What brings you here?" Nick asked.

"I had a little fuel problem heading north toward Seoul and had to check in to K9 East. Mechanics say it looks fixable. I'll be out of here at 0600." Ramón raised his glass. "Sometimes it's good to get stoned with a friend who understands what it's actually like to be in battle." He sat back down. "Then maybe you can talk about what really happened."

Nick smiled. "Seems like you've had a few already, Ray."

Ramón shrugged off the comment, then turned serious. "Look Nick. I know you just came through some serious shit. Looks like you made it OK though. You all right in your head? I mean any lasting effects?"

An image of the screaming NKPA soldier covered in gelatinous flames flashed through Nick's mind. He wrinkled his forehead. "Not particularly," he said.

"Great, buddy." Ramón looked down at his beer. "Been a little rough for me though."

"What's up, Ray?"

"Some of the shit we have to do. Like strafing civilians who won't stop approaching our lines. I've certainly killed a few women and children, Nick."

Nick laid his hand on Ramón's forearm. "Look, man. I'm pretty sure we all have killed innocent people in this war. I can tell you some terrible infantry stories. A lot of innocents get killed when we come through."

Neither man talked for several minutes. Then Ramon broke the ice.

"So. What's it like living here in Busan?"

"Don't really know the place, Ray. But it's heaven if you like seafood."

"Seems like you've got a lot of refugees on the street here."

"Yeah," Nick said." The city's packed with people fleeing the violence. Even the hillside is covered with their campsites." He shrugged. "But we're off again real soon. It's hard to get invested in any one place these days."

Nick looked directly into Ramón's eyes. "You lucky bastard. Living with your wife and kids in a nice air force housing project with a garden, movie theater and a PX. What more could you want?"

"Wait!" Nick realized his half-joking remark was actually a rant. "Sorry, Ray. I *am* happy for you. And Concepción is a gem." He downed another swig of Soju. "Damn. I'm just wish I could be with Ruth now. But it's not in the cards, Ray. We're heading back into it real soon."

"Yeah. Me too, buddy. Maybe I sleep at night with Concepción, but I'm over enemy territory every day."

Nick lowered his voice. "What ops are you flying these days?"

"Mostly supply route interdictions. Some direct ground support north of Daegu. Bombing and strafing tanks and trucks. Napalming enemy troops."He downed another Soju. "Sometimes shooting refugees." Ramón became silent, rimming his Soju glass with a fingertip.

Nick wasn't sure what else to say.

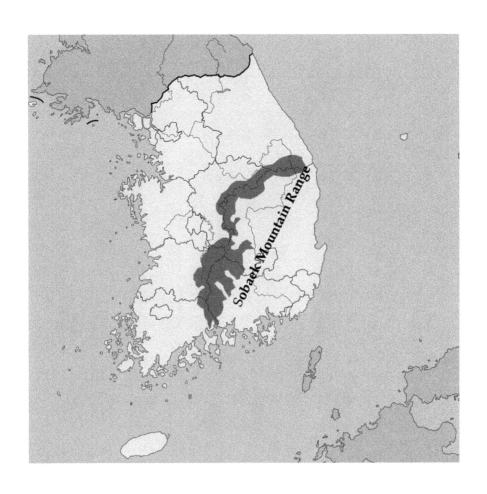

Chapter Nineteen
NKPA Retreats

SEOUL, SOUTH KOREA—*General Douglas MacArthur visited the Han River front today and watched United States Marines clean out north Korean pockets along the stream and on key ridges...General MacArthur said: "You've done a perfect job." Colonel Murray pointed to the hill where the Reds still held out beyond the Han. "They'll all evaporate very shortly," General MacArthur said.*

New York Times
September 21, 1950

Sobaek Mountains, Republic of Korea
September 29, 1950

Ho-jun braced his feet against the floorboard of the doorless, Russian GAZ-67 jeep as SGT Hak accelerated out of a steep curve. The valley road threading between two hillsides was ablaze with the fall colors of larches, maples and oaks— brilliant orange, red and yellow. Ho-jun looked back at the columns of black smoke billowing above the distant tree line. Dug in with camouflaged tanks, antitank guns and extensive mine fields, a valiant NKPA armored division was holding the line east of Daejeon as scattered elements of Ho-jun's 6th

Division dispersed into the craggy Sobaek Mountains of southern Korea.

After the X Corps landing at Incheon, the bloody stalemate along the Busan perimeter had come to an end. The 7th US Army and several attached ROK units were now heading south along a route from Suwon to Daegu. Simultaneously, the 8th US Army was breaking out of the Busan perimeter and advancing north to link up with the southern drive of X Corps. Additional ROK units were advancing from Busan up the east coast of the peninsula.

In disarray, the NKPA 6th Division had broken into smaller units that, although less effective in combat, were better suited to slip between the jaws of the UN pincer movement and escape into the mountains. With US tank battalions biting at their heels, Ho-jun's 6th Division had little time to deploy their usual defensive tactics of laying mine fields or blowing up bridges. They had to move north as rapidly as possible.

Except for SGT Hak, all of Ho-jun's medical treatment squad had been killed or separated from the unit during the desperate escape from the battle along the Nakdong River. Heading deeper into the rugged mountains, Ho-jun and SGT Hak were now relatively safe from attack as they threaded the needle between UN forces sweeping up and down the peninsula.

Ho-jun had mixed emotions. Although he was never convinced that invasion of the South was a wise decision, there certainly was no honor in retreat. Still, it was a relief to be out of the fierce battle zone heading north. In the fresh mountain air beneath a clear azure sky, he imagined himself back in Min-ji's arms.

Ho-jun's brief reverie was interrupted by a small aircraft flying low over the pass. "Spotter!" SGT Hak yelled over the roar of the jeep engine. An icy current of apprehension swept through Ho-jun's body. The reconnaissance plane would certainly locate the brave NKPA armored division that was holding off the American tank battalion. Their sacrifice was making this escape possible.

Soon an B-26 Invader flew low overhead, descending toward Daejeon. Both mesmerized and saddened, Ho-jun turned to watch a large fireball expand in the West, its color shifting from red to yellow as a smoky cloud drifted across the ridges behind them. He was in full retreat while those men were dying for him. It was a sad and dishonorable feeling.

After driving the dark, serpentine road on low beams for several hours, they decided to bivouac until dawn in a small clearing overlooking a ravine. While SGT Hak refilled the gas tank from a jerrycan, Ho-jun stretched in the cold mountain air. Stars, scintillating in the clear night sky, bathed the peaks of the Sobaek Mountains in silver light while the valleys remained blanketed in shadows. Ho-jun sat on a large boulder and slowly scanned the silent horizon. Despite this storm of fire, he loved his beautiful country, both north and south.

September 30, 1950

At dawn, a light frost glistening on the boulders surrounding the jeep began to evanesce with the first golden rays of sunlight. SGT Hak sat down next to Ho-jun and shook his head. "We certainly came close, Comrade Doctor. Victory was right at our fingertips."

Ho-jun nodded silently, his eyes tracking the shadow retreating across the valley floor as the sun rose above the eastern slopes of the range. What else was there to say? The Russians had taught them excellent tactics. And despite American control of the air and sea, the men fought well. But now vastly outnumbered, escape was their only option. He turned to SGT Hak. "Let's get back on the road."

All morning they made good time on the narrow mountain road. Except for an occasional abandoned vehicle, there was little evidence of their 6th Division comrades. Then in mid-afternoon, after crossing an open stretch of road, they came across an NKPA truck riddled with bullet holes that was parked in a clearing shaded by a grove of pine trees.

SGT Hak pulled over behind a small group of NKPA soldiers who were leaning over a young man lying on the ground. "We're a medical team!" SGT Hak called out grabbing the medicine kit. "Can we help?"

A soldier pressing a bloodstained rag against the wounded man's upper arm looked up. "A B-26 caught us in the open." He gestured toward the shattered windshield of the truck. "We can't stop the bleeding."

Ho-jun and SGT Hak knelt down beside the wounded driver who seemed dazed but alert. When Ho-jun removed the blood-soaked bandage, bright red blood pulsed from a large wound below his armpit. Firm pressure with both of Ho-jun's hands failed to stop the bleeding.

"Tourniquet?" SGT Hak asked, opening the medical kit.

Ho-jun nodded, resuming pressure on the wound. "Looks like the axillary artery. It branches up there. Let's hope only one vessel is hit."

SGT Hak wrapped a heavy fiber tourniquet around the upper arm and gradually cinched it tighter with its wooden windlass until the blood ceased pulsing from the wound. He glanced up at Ho-jun who nodded.

"That's about right," Ho-jun said." Let's clean it up and apply a light bandage that can be checked easily. He turned to the wounded man's comrade. "Don't loosen this tourniquet until you reach a hospital."

"Is your truck still running?" SGT Hak asked. One of the soldiers nodded. "Good luck then."

Back on the road, SGT Hak raised his voice above the roaring engine. "It's hard to find a hospital when you're on the run. Won't keeping that tourniquet on cause a lot of damage, Comrade Doctor?"

"Probably," Ho-jun said. "Muscle damage is nearly complete by six hours. He'll likely need an amputation. But it's that or bleed to death."

In the late afternoon, a single-engine, AT-6 Texan buzzed low overhead like a mosquito searching for a blood meal, then climbed and disappeared on the horizon. Ho-jun wasn't worried. They would hardly call in an airstrike for a single jeep on the mountain road. Twisting through the valley, the road ran parallel to a small river. Ho-jun pointed to an unusual rock formation on the riverbank and SGT Hak slowed down. Three boulders had been sculpted into the shape of a turtle. One boulder bore a head with carved eyes, the other two boulders were shaped like flippers.

Ho-jun scanned the hillside above the river. A gravel road led up to an ocher-colored gate, inlaid with a kaleidoscope of multicolored carvings. "That looks like a Buddhist temple," he said. "A good place to rest for the night."

As they approached the entrance of the compound, multi-colored, dragon-like beasts with thick eyelashes and flowing manes carved from wood and stone, emerged from the serpentine surface of the ornate gate. Several monks wearing saffron robes with gray shawls draped across their shoulders gathered around the jeep. Although initially appearing uneasy at the arrival of a military vehicle, the monks soon became hospitable when they learned that Ho-jun and SGT Hak were part of a medical squad. One of the monks was dispatched to inform the Abbot of the monastery.

While SGT Hak secured the equipment in the jeep, a tall monk led Ho-jun into the compound. Passing an intricately carved, five-story pagoda and a ten-meter-tall statue of Buddha with one open palm raised and the other held out in supplication, they ascended a steep, stone staircase. The octangular-temple had a tile roof adorned with ornamental detail of the Silla era. Ho-jun was mesmerized. It was like returning to a kingdom that existed a thousand years in the past.

Inside the temple, apricot-colored rays of the setting sun streamed through windows set high above a corridor lined with gold-plated images of the seated Buddha. At the end of the corridor was a large bronze bell embossed with raised bands and esoteric inscriptions. Before the massive bell stood the Abbot, a balding, man in a gray robe, bowing to his visitor with palms together.

Ho-jun placed his palms flat against his chest and bowed deeply. "Thank you for your hospitality, honorable *Juji*. We'll be gone in the morning."

"You are welcome to stay here as long as you wish," the Abbot said. "Although I suspect you are in a hurry."

Even though Ho-jun was part of an invading army, he felt an aura of compassion emanating from the Abbot. Although not particularly religious, Ho-jun had been raised with deep respect for Confucian ethics—sympathy and good will toward others, a sense of honorable duty and clear moral standards. While many of his countrymen, north and south, had embraced Buddhism or Christianity, the power struggles that often ensued were distressing to Ho-jun.

When he was growing up in colonial Korea, Imperial Japan had imposed Shinto and emperor worship on the population. Now, the current South Korean President Syngman Rhee, a Christian, was attempting to suppress Buddhism. And in the communist north, all religious practices were being discouraged. Nevertheless, the basic tenets of Buddhism sparked Ho-jun's intellectual curiosity.

The Abbot led Ho-jun past a candle-lit altar where a golden statue of Buddha sat before an age-darkened tapestry of multiple, ethereal entities. "Bodhisattvas," the Abbot said. He paused, smiling. "Their mission is to help all sentient beings achieve enlightenment."

The Abbot ushered Ho-jun through a narrow passage that ended at a heavy wooden door. When the Abbot lifted the thick wooden latch and opened the doorway, Ho-jun was astonished to find himself standing at the edge of a well-worn, forest path. Interspersed between towering stalks of bamboo and gracefully bowing spruce, a grove of maple trees was resplendent in its full, fall colors.

Deeper in the forest, a harsh call with a peculiar ascending note emanated from high in the trees. Ho-jun looked up. Two small birds, one black, one white with blue-tinged wings, flitted from branch to branch at the top of a maple tree. "It's a good day for you," the Abbot said. "The magpie brings good fortune." Ho-jun smiled politely. This priest was certainly full of warm aphorisms.

The forest path led to a tiled-roof pavilion on the edge of a small pond. The Abbot gestured toward a wooden bench at the edge of the water. "Please rest for a moment," he said. "I believe you've been on a difficult journey."

When they sat on the bench, a small frog leapt from a mossy boulder into the pond. For several minutes both men sat silently watching the frog's wake undulate in ever-widening circles across the still water. With the musky-sweet smell of fallen leaves suffusing his nostrils, Ho-jun tried to unwrinkle his agitated mind. He'd always loved this time of year. And this tranquil sanctuary was a refreshing respite from the arduous horrors of war.

Allowing his eyes to become unfocused across the still water of the pond, Ho-jun spoke in a low voice. "It *has* been a difficult journey for me, *Juji*." His voice became choked with unanticipated emotion. "I've seen so much death and destruction."

The Abbot sat silently and nodded.

Ho-jun continued. "I've lost many loved ones and I've learned that my own soldiers are killing prisoners and civilians." He shook his head slowly back-and-forth. "I'm a doctor, *Juji*. As a noncombatant, am I acting for the benefit of all people? Am I fighting for a just cause? Is there ever any morality to war?"

The Abbot spoke softly. "I'm just a simple Jogye monk following the Bodhisattva path. I have no special powers nor authority to grant absolution. But I do understand your predicament. As a doctor, I suspect you are inspired to relieve suffering and make things better for others. This is a manifestation of Bodhisattva energy and I commend you for it.

But I believe we are more than individuals in a finite world. Ultimately, there are no individuals, no sentient beings. *We're just a flash of lightning in a summer cloud. A bubble in a stream. This world will pass like a star at dawn.*"

Chapter Twenty
Pyongyang

TOKYO—*UN forces pounding northward to close a new trap on thousands of Communists shoved the enemy back to within 64 miles of Pyongyang Friday after a terrific naval bombardment of the North Korean east coast on a pre-invasion scale.*

Nippon Times
October 14, 1950

Pyongyang, DPRK
October 14, 1950

The retreat from South Korea had been long and hazardous, but Ho-jun and SGT Hak avoided any contact with the enemy. Across the 38th parallel at Cheorwon, they took only backroads on the western side of the Taebaek Mountains until they reached the main highway at Koksan and slipped between the lines of enemy attack. At the approach to Pyongyang, long lines of military vehicles streamed south out of the city. Ho-jun scrutinized the faces of the soldiers as the troop trucks passed by. They looked so young. Barely out of school. Probably just raw recruits.

"They're reinforcements for Kumchon," SGT Hak said, referring to the battle raging at the last major NKPA stronghold, just 140 kilometers south of Pyongyang.

Ho-jun gazed through the arched, steel railing of the Okryu bridge while SGT Hak maneuvered their dusty jeep through the mid-afternoon traffic entering the city. As he watched a small boat churn upstream along the bank of the Taedong River, he felt a release of the persistent tension he'd carried over the past few months. Pleasant memories surged through his body. The last time he was home, the city was blanketed with snow and the river partially frozen over. Now the trees lining the river displayed a brilliant palate of yellow, orange and red leaves. It seemed eons ago since he'd held his wife Min-ji in his arms.

Once over the bridge, they headed down Sungri Street, weaving around fortified barriers manned by NKPA machine gun and mortar teams. Passing between two T-34 tanks placed on either side of an open roadblock, they drove by the ancient Taedong gate and Kim Il-sung Square—the familiar, lunchtime route Ho-jun took when he worked at the University Hospital. In the warm sunshine, only a few pedestrians strolled across the immense square, now flanked by tanks and artillery batteries. Two red banners, each emblazoned with a red star within a white circle, hung over the walls of a government building that faced the square. Directly over the building's entrance was a large portrait of the vigilant *Great Leader*.

In a few more blocks, they turned onto Sosong Street, and shortly arrived at Ho-jun's apartment building on the edge of Kimmy Boi Park. Both SGT Hak, who lived in the working class district of *Potonggang-guyok*, and Ho-jun, who lived in this more fashionable *Chung-guyok* district, were eager to see their families even though they could only stay overnight. Tomorrow they had to continue north to Kanggye, the provisional headquarters of the retreating DPRK.

After SGT Hak drove away, Ho-jun shouldered his battered duffel bag and climbed the stairs to his third floor apartment. Had it really been six months since he last mounted these steps? When he opened the door, he noticed the French impressionist painting on the wall had been replaced with a woodcut of the Bodhisattva *Guanyin*, the goddess of mercy and compassion. Ho-jun smiled to himself. What other changes in decor might Min-ji have made in his absence? He checked his watch. 1500. She wouldn't be home from her teaching job for a couple of hours. He had just enough time to walk through the park to see if Alexei was still at the Russian embassy.

Desiccated leaves, clinging precariously to their branches, shimmied in a gentle breeze on Ho-jun's short walk to the Russian embassy on the other side of the park. The Soviet soldier at the wrought iron gate briefly checked his identification papers and waved him on past a group of men loading crates into covered ZIS-150 trucks. Inside the austere, colonnaded building, embassy staff carried boxes and equipment up and down the marble stairway like army ants on an urgent mission.

At the top of the staircase Ho-jun found Alexei's office door open. *"Privyet, Tovarich!"* he said stepping inside the room. Hello, Comrade.

Alexei looked up from a pile of papers spread across his desk and smiled broadly. "Ho-jun!" He pushed back his chair and hastened across the room to seize his old Korean comrade by the shoulders. "I'm so happy to see you're alive." He ushered Ho-jun inside and closed his office door.

"I'm just passing through on the way to Kanggye," Ho-jun said. He gestured toward the open file cabinets and stacks of papers on the floor. "It looks like you're getting ready to leave."

"I'll be on an Ilyushin transport plane to Moscow tonight." Alexei opened a desk drawer and uncorked a bottle of vodka. "*Na Zdorovie!*" He took a large swig and passed the bottle to Ho-jun. "Sorry, Comrade. I have no glasses."

"*Geonbae!*" Ho-jun returned the toast in Korean and downed the vodka.

Ho-jun was delighted to be with Alexei. The Russian bear and the Korean amur, two old comrades together again. After asking each other about the well-being of their families, they exchanged information about the current status of the war.

"It wasn't a failure of the tactics you Russians taught us," Ho-jun said. "We were actually holding our own until the landing at Incheon."

"A bit like the Greeks at Thermopylae?" Alexei said with a wry smile.

Ho-jun laughed, then turned serious. "I've been on the road for the past month. What's our current status, Alexei?"

"Today's report isn't good. The UN offensive is finally breaking through at Kumchon and ROK forces are closing in from the East. They'll probably form a pincer movement around Pyongyang in the next few days. Marshall Stalin had promised some air support, but it seems that is no longer likely. I'm afraid you're on your own, Comrade. I'm sorry."

On the walk back through the park Ho-jun's thoughts swirled like fallen leaves just before a storm. He'd witnessed the brutality of the Japanese and his own army as an occupying force. What might become of Min-ji and his family when the enemy enters his hometown? Or bombs it? And what could he do about it? Desert and try to protect them? No. He would never abandon his comrades in arms.

Back at the apartment Ho-jun shaved, showered and donned the dark blue, silk robe Min-ji had given him on their first anniversary. As he sat waiting for her to come home, he opened an anthology of Korean poetry she'd left on the low, wooden table. A tattered scrap of paper, tucked between the book's yellowed pages, fluttered to the floor. Scooping up the paper, he beamed. It was the poem he'd written on the road to Kaesong last June. *When we startled the cranes...*

At 1700 Ho-jun's heart leapt when Min-ji opened the apartment door. When she saw Ho-jun, she dropped her bag to the floor. "*Yeobo!*" Tears welled up in her eyes.

Ho-jun rushed to Min-ji, swept aside her respectful bow, and wrapped her in his arms. Min-ji swayed with Ho-jun, her hands around his neck, pulling his lips toward hers. Their fingertips swept up and down each others bodies. Kisses deeper and deeper in ecstatic dance.

After they'd made rapturous love, Ho-jun and Min-ji lay on the futon together, catching their breath. Min-ji turned toward Ho-jun and held his head between her hands. "So much has happened since we were last together. What's it been like for you?"

With all of the horrors he'd seen, Ho-jun wasn't sure how much he would share with Min-ji. "There were some difficult times," he said. "But thoughts of you always kept me going."

Min-ji remained silent for several long moments, then spoke softly. "I understand that you don't want to talk about it now, Ho-jun. I hope someday you'll tell me everything."

Ho-jun nodded. *Everything?* No. There were some things he would never tell her.

Later, over dinner of rice and a meatless, kimchi soup, they talked about the war. "After all our early victories it's a shock to have the enemy at our door," Min-ji said. "I'm frightened."

Ho-jun laid a hand on hers. What could he say? ROK units had often been vindictive when re-capturing lost ground in the South. Maybe the Americans would be different.

"We've been preparing for an invasion," Min-ji said. "Our *inminban* group has organized air raid drills and built dugouts throughout the neighborhood."

Ho-jun smiled dryly. "So, instead of interfering with personal affairs, they've decided to protect citizens? That sounds like an improvement for the *inminban*. What about your school?"

"The young children are mostly confused. Even though official messages have been optimistic, they feel the anxiety. We've moved our classroom into the basement. So far the Americans have only bombed the airfield on the edge of the city. Do you think they'll bomb the center?"

"I doubt it. Killing civilians won't help them take over the city any faster."

Min-ji closed her eyes briefly. "What about the fire bombing of Japanese cities during the last war?"

"That was a different time. And it didn't shorten the war. So far the Americans have only bombed military targets, factories and transportation hubs. Don't worry, *yeobo*. I don't think they'll bomb Pyongyang."

Despite his reassurance, Ho-jun, felt the dark shadow of reality hanging over his transient marital bliss. The enemy was fast approaching Pyongyang and he knew firsthand what an occupying army might do. But there was no other option. He had to leave the one he loved most and rejoin the desperate battle.

October 15, 1950

In the morning, after a brief, bittersweet visit with his parents and sister, Ho-jun and SGT Hak headed 300 kilometers north to the provisional DPRK headquarters in Kanggye, an industrial and timber processing city nestled in the rugged mountains near the Chinese border.

China

Chosin (Changjin) Reservoir

Yellow
Sea

Sea of Japan
(East Sea of Korea)

South Korea

Chapter Twenty One
31st Regimental Combat Team

The battle for Korea is about over. Four months ago this Wednesday the tank-led columns of the North Korean army moved across the 38th parallel. Today that army is destroyed and victory for United Nations forces is at hand in all Korea.

New York Times
October 22, 1950

Off the coast of Iwôn, DPRK
November 3, 1950

At mid-day, with storm clouds looming overhead, Nick took one last drag off his cigarette and flicked it over the chipped railing of the USS General M. M. Patrick. For the past three days the Navy engineers, aided by a helicopter and an underwater demolition team, had been sweeping the approach to the beach at Iwôn to establish a safe landing site. The Navy did not want to repeat the recent mistakes made at Wonsan where two minesweepers were sunk by magnetic mines that had been arrayed, with the assistance of Soviet advisors, in a deadly, sophisticated web.

Here off Iwôn, the Navy minesweepers had conducted an extremely thorough search while the waiting troop transport ships *yo-yo'd* up and down the coast. Now, with the beach declared safe for landing, Nick's 4th platoon of Able Company was preparing to disembark on the hostile coast of North Korea.

Since their withdrawal from the perimeter around Busan, the NKPA had been slowing the northern advance of UN forces with heavily fortified positions. Each step of the way left bloody footprints behind. And last night's briefing with Colonel Allan MacLean, commander of the 31st Regimental Combat Team (RCT-31), was worrisome.

Sketchy reports of a Chinese attack on the US 8th Army in northwestern Korea had been received from X Corps headquarters. Nick felt on edge. It was hard to know what to expect here on an unknown beach in the middle of nowhere.

For the past month in Busan, RCT-31 had been training for a mission in the eastern, coastal range of North Korea. Composed of an artillery company, a tank company and three infantry battalions, RCT-31 was augmented with 300 attached ROK soldiers.

In order to increase the effectiveness of his combat team, Colonel MacLean, a West Point graduate and veteran of the European theater during World War Two, initiated an intense training program. In addition to rigorous physical conditioning, the men of RCT-31 were taught the basics of mountain warfare, fire control, equipment maintenance and communication techniques. When not in training exercises, the combat team had been confined like Spartan warriors to the USS General M. M. Patrick, anchored in Busan harbor.

In the late afternoon, the LVT carrying Nick's platoon traversed back and forth off the beach for two hours while army engineers used bulldozers to stabilize the soft sand with inland soil and construct ramps to allow the transports to unload directly onto the beach. Crammed like a sardine between 25 men in the cold, steel compartment of the amphibious landing craft, Nick became chilled by the steady rain working its way through the collar of his poncho. He turned to SGT Miller. "Jesus, Mike. I'm freezing my ass off out here."

"Hang on, Lieutenant," Miller said. "Things will heat up soon enough."

As the LVT churned through the water waiting for the engineers to complete their work, Nick had plenty of time to evaluate the coastline which lay barren and bleak in the rain beneath a range of saw-toothed peaks.With no obvious sign of resistance, Nick remained vigilant. Although on its heels, the NKPA was putting up one hell of a fight. There had been nothing obvious at Wonsan either—just before the snipers came out.

Because the sand on the beach provided little traction for most vehicles, tanks were off-loaded first and used like tractors to haul the trucks and artillery ashore. Then came the men of RCT-31 splashing through the water, crouched low with their rifles held high. Hitting the sand, Nick's heart was pounding like a runaway train as he focused on the rise beyond the shoreline. Mortars, small arms and machine gun fire could rake the landing force at any moment.

But there was no enemy fire on the desolate beach. Only the menacing sounds of the LVTs like mighty beasts clawing their way out of the ocean onto land. Roaring, clanking and whirring across the sand, the vehicles of RCT-31 belched dark clouds of smoke into the falling rain. Soon the convoy was heading north into the mountains, tasked with guarding the left flank of the 17th Infantry Regiment as it drove to capture the crossroads town of Kapsan.

Fusen Reservoir
November 15, 1950

Nick's body vibrated with the jeep's chassis over each bump as SGT Miller maneuvered along the narrow, mountainous road south of the Fusen Reservoir. Created to harness hydroelectric power, the finger-like reservoir was one of several built in northern Korea by the Imperial Japanese during their half century of colonization.

Enveloped in the incessant roar of the convoy and the rhythmic thrum of the Jeep's 4-cylinder engine, Nick sat silently scanning the landscape. When they'd sailed from Busan at the end of October, the leaves of the maple and oak trees had displayed an astonishing variety of brilliant colors. But here in the mountains of North Korea most of the fall colors had faded into brown and pale yellow—the leaves of birch and larch trees twisted and dangling from barren branches, silhouetted against the cold, gray sky. At night subzero temperatures caused his M1 Carbine to function poorly. Ammunition rounds failed to feed. The bolt wouldn't close. If the rifle did fire, it had little stopping power. Nick switched to the trusty M1 Garand.

At 1700, just before sunset, Nick's platoon set up a roadside bivouac beside a clear, mountain stream. About six feet wide, the fast-flowing stream snaked through a small, rocky valley carved between the steep, pine-forested slopes of the Taebaek Mountains. While the men of his platoon set up defensive perimeters and improvised hooches from tarps and ponchos, Nick sat in an officer's meeting with his battalion commander Lieutenant Colonel (LTC) Don Carlos Faith.

"So far, so good," said LTC Faith, a tall, handsome infantry officer who'd received two bronze stars during World War Two for airborne jumps in Africa, Italy, France, Holland and Germany. "But we are definitely out on a limb here. Be doubly sure your boys are vigilant tonight. After the attack on the 8th Army in the northwest, we need to be wide awake." He turned to the Captain Ed Stamford, a Marine air controller attached to RCT-31. "Tell them what you heard today, Ed."

Stamford shifted his muscular frame on the empty ammunition box he was using for a stool and took a large slug of his coffee. "One of the Corsair pilots radioed they'd detected some action below the Chosin Reservoir yesterday. Looks like the 1st Marines engaged some enemy troops near the Funchilin Pass."

"North Koreans?" Able Company commander CPT Ed Steward asked.

"The Corsair pilot was flying too high to say," Stamford said. "But the attackers were wearing white uniforms."

"Sounds like the Chinese," Faith said. "But it's hard to know how many. G2 says there are only a few volunteers in the area." He stood tall. "Ok. That's all. Try to get some rest. We'll shove off at dawn."

Back at his bivouac site by the mountain stream, Nick ducked beneath the barren limbs of a wild mulberry tree and stepped onto the bank at the edge of the water. Walking through the squishy sedge, he sat on a boulder and trailed his fingers in the frigid mountain stream. *Only a few Chinese volunteers?* He recalled the reduced numbers of enemy troops that Willoughby reported to SCAP in Tokyo. In the field, he would never rely on G2 estimates.

Something soft brushed across Nick's cheek; then another lit on his nose. In the fading twilight, snowflakes fell silently from a stratus cloud spreading like a dark blanket over the valley. A gust of bone chilling wind rifled through Nick's fatigue jacket. Here in the rugged mountains of North Korea, over 60 miles distant from other UN forces, Nick felt the same bleak isolation he'd known as a youth, snowshoeing high above the tree line in the Cascades. There was both beauty and danger in that feeling.

Rustling through the reeds like a cautious predator, 2nd LT. Lee, commander of the ROK troops attached to RCT-31, stepped onto the bank beside Nick. "Sorry to disturb your meditation, Lieutenant. Just reporting my men are now 100 meters east of your platoon."

Pffft. Something rustled in the underbrush beneath the pine trees along the slope of the mountains. Then a small, brown deer with a thick coat, fur-covered ears and prominent tusks instead of antlers, bounded across the stream.

"What the hell was that?" Nick said. "Looked like Dracula."

"A water deer," LT Lee said. "No deer in Oregon?"

"Yeah, but a lot bigger. And no fangs," Nick said.

"Strange," LT Lee said, scanning the slopes. "Why would deer run toward us?"

A shrill whistle echoed through the forest. Then men in white quilted uniforms rushed out of the trees just 50 yards away. Firing burp guns and vintage Russian carbines, a dozen

Chinese soldiers charged the men of Nick's platoon who were busy spreading out tarps for the night or heating rations over their Coleman stoves.

LT Lee immediately opened fire with his M1, taking one Chinese soldier down. A lightning bolt of energy shot through Nick's body. He raised his rifle and released the safety. Too many Chinese. Not enough time. But before he got off a shot, Browning automatic rifle fire erupted from a sentry post on the platoon's perimeter. Then concentrated fire poured in from the rifle team posted on the opposite side of their bivouac. Three, then four more Chinese attackers fell.

Nick shot one of the four remaining enemy soldiers who was attacking Lee with his bayonet. With no time to fix his own bayonet, Nick pulled the K-bar knife from the sheath on his belt and parried the thrust of a brawny, Chinese soldier's bayonet with his forearm while simultaneously stomping on his shin bone with a heavy combat boot. Nick felt time slowing down as he reflexively flowed into the *Kempo* combat techniques he'd practiced with great diligence since his lessons at Fort Lewis. Stiff arming the Chinese soldier who was grasping frantically at his shoulder, Nick plunged the K-bar deep into his neck, and yanked it back with savage force.

While Lt Lee was engaged in hand-to-hand combat with one of the Chinese attackers, the remaining one rushed forward, tugging on the igniter cord of a Type 67 stick grenade. When the Chinese soldier cocked his arm to heave the grenade toward the platoon, Nick cut him down with a burst from his M1 Garand.

Nick turned to help LT. Lee who had his attacker pinned to the ground with his body lying across the chest, an elbow pressing into his neck and one arm locked around his wrist. Nick pressed his rifle against the Chinese soldier's head. His finger gripped the trigger, then relaxed. The lightning energy coursing through his body subsided into a steady stream of vigilance. These weren't Japs who'd always fight to the death. Like the North Koreans, the Chinese were fierce warriors but would probably surrender when it was clear that all was lost. Lee stood up as riflemen from the platoon ran over to take charge of the prisoner.

Nick extended a hand to help LT Lee off the ground. "Jiu-jitsu, eh?" He said as they walked back up the slope to the road. "I saw some of that on New Guinea."

LT Lee smiled. "I have good training from the Imperial Japanese Army." He stopped walking. "But don't worry. Our Gando Special Force fought bandits and communist guerrillas in Manchukuo. Not Americans in New Guinea."

The Chinese attack killed two men in Nick's 4th platoon and wounded another. With LT. Lee translating from Mandarin to English, LTC Faith joined Nick and Able Company commander CPT Steward to interrogate the prisoner. Calm and rugged, the Chinese soldier said he was a veteran of the Manchurian campaign against Imperial Japan.

How ironic. A Chinese communist veteran being interrogated by a Korean officer who had once been in the Imperial Japanese Army. Half a decade ago, Nick's current enemy would have been his ally while his current ally would have been the enemy.

"What unit are you from?" Faith asked the Chinese soldier through LT Lee.

"80th Division, 9th People's Volunteer Army," the Chinese soldier said without hesitation. "We've come to help liberate the people of Korea."

"How large is your force?" Faith asked.

"Ten divisions in this sector."

After the prisoner was led away, Faith turned to LT Lee. "Think he's telling the truth?"

"I'm not sure, Colonel" LT Lee said. "Maybe trying to scare us?"

Faith glanced at Nick and CPT Steward.

"I don't know, sir," Nick said. "He seemed surprisingly open."

"So much for name, rank and serial number," CPT Steward said. "And what's this "volunteer" army?"

"Calling themselves volunteers doesn't change anything. They're regular Chinese People's Liberation Army," Faith said.

"Ten divisions, sir?" Steward said.

"That would more than 100,000 men," Faith said. "We have no intel suggesting that many Chinese are in Korea."

Nick felt a shiver down his spine. *Intel from Willoughby? Christ.* Nick remained silent.

Taebaek Mountain Range

Chapter Twenty Two
Into the unknown

TOKYO—*The advance of the United Nations troops to the Yalu River on the northeastern front in the Korean fighting emphasizes the determination of the United Nations to complete its mission against aggression in Korea despite the invasion of Korean territory by the Chinese Communists.*

Nippon Times
November 23, 1950

Taebaek Mountains DPRK
November 25, 1950

In-mid-morning, the sun was beginning to break through a smoky haze above the snow-capped Taebaek range as SGT Miller expertly maneuvered their Willy's MB jeep on the rutted mountain road. Jolting and sliding through a gauntlet of ruts and glazed frost patches, bone-dry snow mixed with frozen dirt and gravel shot from the jeep's sturdy rear tires into the subzero air. On one side of the perilous route, were boulders blanketed with thick layers of ice and snow. The other side plummeted toward the frozen reservoir below. The Koreans called it the *Changjin* Reservoir. But the U.S.military had only out-dated Japanese maps. So *Chosin* Reservoir it was for the Army.

Nick glanced at his wristwatch. 1130. Not bad. He released the coiled-tension in his body. This time of year the sun set about 1630 in the mountains. They'd probably be able to bivouac on the northeast side of the reservoir before dark. He sure as hell didn't want his battalion to be on the road after sundown. That's when the white-quilted Chinese were likely to spring into action. The PLA prisoner at the Fusen Reservoir claimed the PLA had ten divisions operating in the area. In contrast, G2 staff estimated that only a few Chinese "volunteers" were in the region.

Nick inhaled deeply through his nostrils and blew out an impressive cloud of steam that lingered a few moments around his face before dissolving into the frigid air. Whatever their numbers, Chinese soldiers were avoiding the roads and traveling through the mountains at night carrying only essential supplies on their backs. The rumor was they hid in shallow trenches at daybreak and covered their white uniforms with fresh snow. Maybe they did. Who knew what was true or just a rumor these days? He swept his gaze across the landscape. Nothing moving.

Nick glanced at LT Lee and CPT Steward who were bundled in blankets, parkas, ponchos and scarves over their heavy winter uniforms in the back of the canvas-topped Jeep. Exposed to the fierce Arctic cold, Steward's face, had become alabaster white. Lee's darker face had turned a bronze color that accentuated the pale scar running across his cheek. Nick turned away. No use talking, nor even shouting. The clacking whine of the Jeep's straight-four Go Devil engine, straining downhill in second gear, made conversation almost impossible.

A beam of sunlight, muted by streaming clouds, swept across the barren ridgeline. These mountains were not like the densely forested ones at home in Oregon. Here in the high mountains of northern Korea, the hillsides were studded with plenty of boulders, but only a few scraggly pines. And this time of year, most winter nights brought a bone-chilling wind out of Manchuria with temperatures plunging as low as -40°F. Vehicles were kept idling all night. Rifles and automatic weapons were fired intermittently to to keep them from freezing up. But most important, numb and tingling fingers and toes, passed through a spectrum of red, white and blue before hardening into the yellow-gray hue of severe frostbite.

Nick grasped the ends of his wool scarf between his Arctic glove mittens and tightened it higher on the bridge of his nose. Wasn't this a kick in the ass? He'd thought nothing could be worse than fighting the Japs in the steamy jungles of the Pacific or trying to dig a trench on a coral reef as tracers zinged overhead. It was the soldier's eternal question—if not killed in action, would you rather die of thirst or be frozen to death? With the blanket wrapped firmly around his parka, he pressed his back against the seat and shifted his weight with each bounce as the sturdy Jeep made its way down the pass toward the reservoir.

Nick was uneasy. Except for the rumbling roar of the convoy, the mountains seemed deathly quiet. Something wasn't quite right. X Corps demands for a speedy advance toward the Yalu River seemed reckless. And this mission, taking point at the northeastern bank of the reservoir, would thrust his battalion out on a very precarious limb. Back in Tokyo, MacArthur was certain the Chinese wouldn't come in to this war. Nick wasn't so sure. But what the hell? He was only a First Lieutenant. What could he do?

Two days ago, as a reward for pushing the NKPA up to the Manchurian border, Nick's unit enjoyed a Thanksgiving bivouac feast courtesy of the brass. Nick wanted to believe MacArthur's promise to pull out before Christmas. He yearned to be with Ruth back in their Tokyo quarters—her warm body lying close to his. But, gorged on turkey, mashed potatoes and apple pie, he knew the job wasn't done. There would still be the cleanup of the ragged, but feisty NKPA all the way up to the border with China. And Christ. What would happen if China came in full bore?

A week ago, with the vanquished NKPA on the run, General Almond and his senior X Corps officers took a ritual victory piss in the Yalu River, the border between Korea and Manchuria. Nick pondered the question ROK Lt. Lee had posed the other night. How would *we* feel if the Chinese marched straight up through Mexico and took a piss in the Rio Grande? Nick pondered the question for a moment, then let it go. *FIGMO—fuck it, I've got my orders*: attack the flank of the shadowy Chinese forces fighting the 8th Army 120 clicks west of here. It would only be a brief bivouac at the reservoir before moving on.

Radio communication in the Taebaek Mountain range was terrible. There were no land lines between units and, to make things worse, the Army and Marine radios were set to operate on different frequencies. Incoming battle reports from the northwestern part of the country were very sketchy. All Nick knew was the Chinese launched a night-time attack against the 8th Army a few days ago, then disappeared by daybreak. But information he gleaned from staff meetings suggested casualties were heavy. Nevertheless, headquarters G2 still claimed only a small group of "Korean volunteers in Chinese uniforms" were operating in the region.

Nick was worried. X Corps, consisting of the 1st Marine Division and two Army divisions, was virtually isolated from the remainder of UN forces in Korea. And now, his battalion's mission was to relieve the Marines dug in along the shore of the reservoir. When the Marines moved out, only Nick's battalion would remain along the east side of the reservoir until the rest of the 31st Regimental Combat Team (RCT-31) arrived.

A lacy veil of snow gliding down a nearby hillside sent a shiver down his spine. Our forces were spread out dangerously thin on a relentless drive toward the border of China.

Chapter Twenty Three
Deep in the Mountains

TOKYO—*Communist resistance melted away before hard-hitting Yank and South Korean infantry and Marine war planes on the northeastern front Saturday, and a X Corps spokesman said there appeared to be no strong enemy forces between them and the Manchurian and Russian borders.*

Nippon Times
November 19, 1950

Kanggye, DPRK
November 25, 1950

At 0700 sunlight reflected off the frosted windows of the NKPA military hospital, high up on the hill. Dr. Choi Ho-jun of the NKPA trudged through the snow on his way to morning rounds with his Chinese PLA colleague Dr. Zhang Liang. Although the recent American fire bombing raid destroyed more than half of the city, this neighborhood, although layered with ash, was still intact. The hospital was the primary referral center for Chinese and North Korean troops fighting in the mountains near the border of China. As was the practice at the time, neither Chinese nor North Korean officers bore military rank. Medical officers were simply addressed as Comrade Doctor.

Ho-jun examined the ink mark he'd drawn yesterday on the leg of a brawny Chinese infantryman. Although the mark, demarcating the advance of damaged tissue, had receded toward the soldier's foot by almost five centimeters, several deep, hemorrhagic blisters remained. He glanced at Dr. Zhang who nodded slightly. "The frostbite is not as far up your leg now," Ho-jun said to the soldier in Chinese. "Where are you from?"

The soldier's eyes widened. "You speak excellent Mandarin, Comrade Doctor. I'm from Shandong Province."

"Shandong?" Ho-jun smiled. "I suspect you're used to a warmer climate," he said with only a slight Korean accent. "I picked up a few words of your language in Manchuria fighting the Japanese alongside my Chinese comrades." He nodded toward Dr. Zhang. "You're making progress, Comrade . We'll examine you again tomorrow morning."

The soldier lowered his head respectfully. "Can you save my foot, Comrade Doctor?"

Ho-jun glanced at the Korean charge nurse whose lips curved subtly downward. "You're doing well," he said in a voice mixed with caution and optimism. "We'll see how your leg looks tomorrow."

"He's going to lose that foot," Dr. Zhang said once they'd left the ward.

At noon, Ho-jun sat with Dr. Zhang at a table in the physician's lounge on the top floor of the hospital, rolling tobacco into cigarettes with strips of the *Rodong Sinmun,* the official newspaper of the Korean Workers' Party. Sealing the paper with his tongue, he offered a cigarette to Dr. Zhang and lit it with a flip-top lighter embossed with the red white and blue image of the DPRK flag. The acrid smell of strong tobacco filled the air.

"The rumor is there'll soon be a major offensive at the Changjin Reservoir," Dr. Zhang said. "We'll probably need to establish a field hospital close to the action. I'd expect a lot of casualties. But I think our consolidated medical team can manage this well together."

"We're short on most supplies, Comrade teacher," Ho-jun said, addressing his medical mentor with appropriate respect. "I'm afraid we're going to have to be innovative."

"Like we were against the Japanese in Manchukuo, eh?"

Ho-jun chuckled. "You certainly showed me how to do a lot with very few resources then, Comrade teacher."

"Well, I hope we're a little more sophisticated now."

Ho-jun looked at his watch. "We'd better get down to the trauma ward. Our *Great Leader* will soon arrive to make rounds and bolster morale."

Dr. Zhang crinkled his eyes with faint amusement. "When did he start calling himself that?"

"About a year ago." Ho-jun smiled. "Perhaps a bit like your *Great Helmsman* Mao?"

Dr. Zhang glanced across the room at a few North Korean doctors in tall, white caps busy in conversation. "Be careful, Comrade. Most people don't know Kim like we do."

Ho-jun nodded and lowered his voice. "The stories of his heroic leadership of the Northeast anti-Japanese Army are a little exaggerated, don't you think? I mean…"

Dr. Zhang cut him off with a wave of his hand as a few more physicians entered the room. "He was a good guerrilla fighter and he's pulled your country together."

Ho-jun smiled. "Yes, but without you Chinese we'd be swimming in the Yalu right now."

Dr. Zhang rose from the table. "Enough politics. Let's get down there and help boost morale." He grasped Ho-jun's arm and whispered in his ear. "Just be careful, Ho-jun. These are dangerous times."

Just as Ho-jun had anticipated, the chubby, youthful-appearing Kim Il-Sung burst onto the hospital ward with all the flourish of the Great Leader he was acclaimed to be. Dressed in a dark blue, Mao-style suit with a DPRK flag pinned to his tunic, Kim strode up to the two white-coated doctors and bowed respectfully to each. "It is a great pleasure to see you once again, Comrade Doctors. May I visit some of the Korean patients?"

Ho-jun looked about the hospital ward, filled with seriously wounded men—Chinese soldiers outnumbered the Koreans 2 to 1. The NKPA was still putting up significant resistance, but most of the wounded were among Chinese PLA pouring into the region under the disingenuous title of the People's *Volunteer* Army. Ho-jun ushered Kim to the bedside of a young NKPA soldier with an above-the-knee amputation. The soldier, shocked to see the Great Leader in person, snapped to attention so smartly that he almost fell off the corner of his bed.

The Great Leader reached out and grasped the young man's arm, settling him back down on his hospital bed. "Your bravery has honored our country," Kim said as he grasped the medal his aide slipped into his hand. He smiled and bent forward to pin a red star with silver-gold wings to the soldier's hospital gown.

Kim's visit was brief and professional. He visited all the Korean patients on the ward and handed out several medals for gallantry. Although Ho-jun had served with Kim in Manchuria, he had never really known him personally. And, despite Kim's greeting of familiarity, it was doubtful that Kim even recalled who he was. But Ho-jun was beginning to understand Kim's grasp of power. Certainly most of it was dictatorial. Any serious opposition was rewarded with imprisonment or death. But the soldiers he visited on the ward were genuinely ecstatic to see the Great Leader. Kim's power came from the people who believed in him—the long-awaited, virtuous Great Leader who would reunite, protect and elevate the pure Korean race.

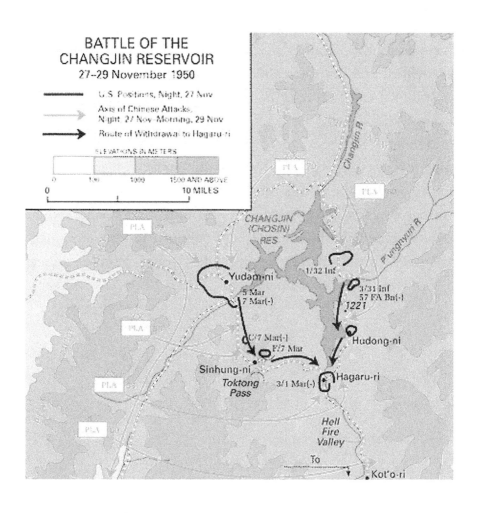

BATTLE OF THE CHANGJIN RESERVOIR
27–29 November 1950

U.S. Positions, Night, 27 Nov

Axis of Chinese Attacks,
Night, 27 Nov–Morning, 29 Nov

Route of Withdrawal to Hagaru-ri

ELEVATIONS IN METERS

| 0 | 500 | 1000 | 1500 AND ABOVE |

0 ——————— 10 MILES

PLA

Changjin R

P'ungnyuri R

CHANGJIN
(CHOSIN)
RES

PLA

PLA

Yudam-ni

5 Mar
7 Mar(-)

1/32 Inf

3/31 Inf
57 FA Bn(-)
1221

PLA

C/7 Mar(-)
F/7 Mar

Hudong-ni

Sinhung-ni
Toktong
Pass

3/1 Mar(-)

Hagaru-ri

PLA

Hell
Fire
Valley

To

Kot'o-ri

Chapter Twenty Four
Chosin Reservoir

TOKYO—There have been no big battles in the far north this week but many encounters. The mountains—some peaks rise to 6,000 feet—forbid mass actions. The roads are described by the Army as "almost impassable," but our men and vehicles have been advancing along them in snow, subzero temperatures and howling winds.

New York Times
November 25, 1950

Hagaru-ri, Korea
November 25, 1950

In mid-afternoon, the temperature was hovering in the high 20s as Nick's 1/32 IN battalion neared the southern tip of the Chosin Reservoir. Shaped on the map like an exotic beast rearing up on its hind legs, the Japanese-made reservoir was bordered east and west by low mountains.

The snow-packed, dirt and gravel road drummed on the undercarriage of Nick's jeep as it churned its wheels in icy ruts that tore at its rugged snow tires. Pumping his legs against the vibrating metal floor to keep his circulation moving, Nick wrapped the head scarf tighter beneath his helmet and rubbed the outer shell of his trigger-finger mittens together. Despite woolen underwear, two pairs of socks, woolen shirt and trousers beneath his cotton field uniform, a pile fleece jacket and a wind resistant parka, there was no escape from the Arctic cold. A bitter chill crept in through every vulnerable entrance. Up his sleeve, around his scarf, his collar, up his pant legs. And this was still mid-afternoon. With the wind out of Siberia tonight, it'll probably be 30-40 below.

The 1/32 IN convoy passed through the raised barricade at the 1st Marine checkpoint just south of the Chosin Reservoir. Nick returned the salutes of the two military policeman in heavy parkas standing between a sand-bagged machine gun nest on one side of the road and a M46 Patton tank on the other. *Poor bastards. Freezing their asses off.* Then again, tonight they'll be in warm bunks, and we'll be bivouacked along the frigid, reservoir road.

The men of Nick's 4th platoon were experienced and competent warriors. Most of the riflemen, light machine gunners and mortar men had been through Incheon. And because of his First SGT Mike Miller, this unit was tight. Nick felt their loyalty and courage. Despite the cold, morale was pretty high. The enemy was on the run. Home by Christmas. That's what MacArthur said.

Despite all the optimism regarding an early victory, Nick remained vigilant. He'd fought against a crafty and powerful Japanese enemy in the Pacific War. And he'd just skirmished with a few bold Chinese at the Fusen Reservoir. Were the Chinese advancing or trying to cover their retreat? Were those kamikaze-like Chinese attackers really a squad from an entire division? A blast of Arctic wind off the reservoir trailed icy fingertips across Nick's neck. *How many Chinese are out there?*

The tents, vehicles, artillery, barrels and stacks of supplies of the 1st Marine Division were scattered like a squalid, Hooverville encampment on the northern edge of the tiny village of Hagaru-ri. SGT Miller shook his head. "Goddam leathernecks. No style at all." But Nick was glad the Marines were around. Unlike many army draftees, they were highly trained and tightly disciplined volunteers. *Gung ho.* Just the kind of guys you need in a pinch.

SGT Miller tapped Nick on his shoulder and pointed toward a motor pool of damaged vehicles. Huddled around a portable, liquid-fuel stove, were a dozen white quilted, Chinese Communist POWs. Two military policemen guarding the prisoners alternated warming their hands over a small, wood fire. Nick felt a tightness in his jaw. The Chinese infantryman who attacked them at the Fusen Reservoir said there were ten divisions in the area. Maybe he was trying to scare us. But were these POWs just stragglers or part of a larger Chinese unit?

On the perimeter of the Marine camp, mortar emplacements surrounded bulldozers and tractors putting the final touches on a recently constructed runway that could accommodate a C-47 transport aircraft. Modified with a reinforced fuselage and a large cargo door, the C-47 could carry up to 6,000 pounds of cargo. Nick rubbed his hands together and stared at the runway. The C-47 could carry a jeep, a cannon or a platoon of soldiers in full combat gear. Looking up at the mountain ridges rising east and west of the reservoir,

Nick's thoughts darkened. The C-47 could also be used to evacuate the seriously wounded—and the dead.

Two Marines in a jeep mounted with a machine gun blocked the beginning of the narrow, dirt road, barely wide enough for the trucks that were heading up the east side of the reservoir. One side of the snowy road was lined with a shallow ravine that rose steeply up the side of a mountain to a ridgeline about 100 feet above the roadbed. The other side of the road dropped precipitously toward the reservoir. Nick recalled LTC Faith's briefing. The reservoir's frozen solid enough to hold a jeep, the Battalion's S2 intelligence officer said. *But what about a jeep crashing onto the ice from above?*

Tipping his helmet in a good luck salute, the Marine driver backed his jeep into a small siding carved out of the steep, rocky slope and waved the convoy on through.

The road north along the east side of the reservoir crossed over numerous, frozen streams, wound around large inlets, and passed over smaller ones on wooden bridges. Halfway up the 15 mile route to the Pungnyuri inlet, the convoy had to ford a stream beneath a concrete bridge that had been blown by the unseen enemy. Nick felt a sour taste in his mouth. Were the Chinese retreating or setting a trap?

It was late afternoon when 1/32 IN bivouacked just south of the 5th Marine Regiment in a small valley at the foot of the 3900 foot Hill 1221. Nick was worried. X Corps forces were spread thinly on low ground between mountain ridges on both sides of the reservoir.

In the evening Nick went with his company commander Captain Steward and battalion commander LTC Faith to an officers meeting with Colonel Murray, the commander of the

5th Marines. Nick found COL Murray to be competent and helpful—a lot like his Dad had been on the farm in Dufur.

"Refugees moving south report a lot of Chinese soldiers just north of us," COL Murray said. "Some POWs claim that three Chinese army divisions are preparing to attack. My Marines have had a few firefights with the Chinese while on reconnaissance patrol, but no major engagements."

COL Murray stood tall and pulled on his helmet. "Be cautious at night, men. You won't see them in the daylight."

November 26, 1950

Shortly after midnight, Nick and Sergeant Miller inspected their platoon's positions below Hill 1221. "I heard some Marine scuttlebutt today," SGT Miller said. "Last night a Marine rifleman was actually pulled from his foxhole and beaten by Chinese soldiers. *Sonofabitch.* They took his rifle, but left him alive."

"Damn! Not like fighting the Japs, is it?" Nick said.

Miller snorted in agreement. "Maybe these Chinks are just trying to warn us, Lieutenant. Give us one last chance to back off." Miller suddenly stopped and spun around. "Where the hell are our sentries?"

Nick and SGT Miller strode through their 4th platoon positions like angry Furies. Only one man was awake. Machine gun positions were not well-aligned and a few hastily dug fox holes were outside the designated line of defense. "Dammit, Mike," Nick said. "Let's kick some ass here." In response, SGT Miller organized walking security patrols and assigned latrine digging duty to a few offenders.

In the morning the 5th Marine Regiment deployed to the west side of the Chosin Reservoir to rejoin their 1st Marine Division. Moving in to the Marine's abandoned positions on Hill 1221, Nick's battalion now stood alone in the Arctic cold south of the Pyungnuri Inlet.

Later that morning the 7th Division Assistant Commander Brigadier General Henry Hodes arrived at LTC Faith's command post on Hill 1221. After flying in to the Marine base at Hagaru-ri from X Corps headquarters near the coast at Hungnam, BG Hodes had driven north by jeep. At the officer's briefing, Nick found BG Hodes to be straightforward and clear. Known as *Hammering Hank*, Hodes was a twice-wounded, combat veteran of World War II who now served as the eyes and ears of the 7th Division Commander Major General David Barr.

"Colonel MacLean's 3/31 Infantry Battalion will be arriving soon along with a heavy mortar company, field artillery battalion and a tank company," BG Hodes said to LTC Faith. "The 2/31 should arrive before we push off on the 28th. MacLean will take the lead for further RCT-31 operations here."

"What's our plan of attack, General?" Faith asked.

"The Marines will be attacking northwest on the 27th. Your RCT-31 will attack north on the 28th," BG Hodes said.

"With a little artillery and tank support from the Marines, we're ready to go right now, General," Faith said.

BG Hodes shook his head. "The orders stand. Wait for MacLean."

After BG Hodes departed, Nick wondered about Faith's bold request. He'd always considered Faith to be courageous and a stand-up commander, but this suggestion seemed reckless. His unit was already way out on a limb. Of *course* they should wait for the full force of RCT-31 to arrive. What the hell was Faith thinking? Thank God for the clear-headed Hodes.

At noon LTC Faith, along with his company commanders and platoon leaders, reconnoitered the abandoned forward Marine positions. "Tell me what you think," Faith asked.

Nick looked up at the forested, eastern mountain ridge rising above their position and shook his head. "This is pretty low ground we're on, sir."

"Won't see much coming down the ridge after dark, sir," CPT Steward said.

"Here between the reservoir and the mountains, our perimeter is much tighter than standing ops," LTC Anderson, the S3 operations officer added.

"We'll be out of here soon enough," Faith said. "Get your boys ready to move north on the 28th."

Throughout the day the men of 1/32 IN alternated between performing their duties and taking a 20 minute break in the warming tents. Digging trenches in the frozen soil was difficult for the first ten inches, but easy in the deeper, rock-free soil. Fire lines were cleared of scrub brush in front of heavy and light weapons squad positions. Maintenance of vehicles and equipment was performed, and supplies were replenished.

In the late afternoon many of the men were sharpening their bayonets as Nick walked through his platoon to the perimeter of their defensive position. Somewhere along the shoreline below a loon chanted its mournful, two-note call.

The Arctic air burned in Nick's nostrils, infusing his upper chest with an unusual tightness. Now that the Marines were gone, 1/32 IN stood alone with no artillery support, squeezed between the ominous mountains and the frozen reservoir.

At 1900 Colonel Allan MacLean, commander of RCT-31, arrived by jeep at Faith's command post on Hill 1221. MacLean, a robust 43-year-old former tackle on the West Point football team, was known for his dynamic personality and uncompromising will to get things done.

Unlike LTC Faith, who had parachuted into many WWII battles, Maclean was a communications and logistics staff officer. He had no combat experience before assuming command of the 31st Infantry Regiment in the battle for Seoul. During the skirmishes at the Fusen Reservoir Nick noticed that MacLean, commander of the newly formed RCT-31, often appeared up front. MacLean was a man who always seemed to be looking for action.

Late in the evening, COL MacLean held an officers meeting in the dusty farmhouse that served as Faith's command post on Hill 1221. "My 3rd Infantry Battalion should be here in the morning along with artillery, mortars and tanks," MacLean said. "The 2nd Infantry Battalion is still on the road but should arrive by late afternoon. Regardless of what forces we have on hand, we'll attack north on the morning of November 28." He glanced at LTC Faith. "Your battalion will spearhead the attack, Don."

"Very good, sir," Faith said. "In preparation for the attack, I'd like to move my battalion to the forward position the Marines just abandoned." He spread a map of the terrain on the tabletop and, pointed to a position north of the Pungnyuri inlet.

To Nick's consternation, MacLean approved the request. *What the hell? This is crackers.* Sending a single battalion forward of its strong defensive position on Hill 1221 before the artillery and armor arrive? MacLean's aggressiveness and Faith's ambition were putting their unit in danger. But *FIGMO.* Nothing to do but follow them.

Chapter Twenty Five
People's Volunteer Army Attacks

SEOUL, Korea—*Chinese Communist troops who helped stall the United Nations drive in central Korea yesterday are being reinforced from an estimated force of 400,000 now massed on the Manchurian side of the Yalu River, intelligence reports to the South Korean Home Ministry said today.*

New York Times
November 27, 1950

Chosin Reservoir
November 27, 1950

By early evening most of the RCT-31 forces had arrived and established positions 3-4 miles south of MacLean's headquarters which was halfway between Hill 1221 and the inlet. The deployment included two infantry battalions, three field artillery batteries, an anti-aircraft battery (used mainly to stem frontal enemy assaults), a heavy mortar company and one tank company. With unreliable wire and radio reception, communications with X Corps headquarters were sporadic. The exact location of the 2/31 IN Battalion was unclear—they were presumed to be traveling north toward the reservoir on the main supply route from the coast.

For an hour after darkness fell, RCT-31 artillery and mortar batteries fired rounds to register the range and accuracy of their weapons. Then there was only the sound of tents flapping in the Arctic wind swirling off the reservoir.

At 2100 LTC Faith met with his company and platoon leaders at his forward command post in an abandoned farmhouse 300 feet south of the northern, defensive perimeter. "I've just returned from meeting with Colonel MacLean," Faith said, spreading a map on the table. "We're set to advance north tomorrow morning. Here's how we're lined up currently." He pointed to positions on the map. "1/31 and the 31st Tank Company are about 10 clicks south of 3/31 along the inlet. Field artillery and anti-aircraft batteries are in place between 3/31 and the tanks. And we're here—5 clicks north of the inlet. The tankers will move up at dawn to advance north with us. Any questions?"

CPT Steward raised a hand. "What's the latest intel, sir?"

"The field wire's down again. But all of the units arriving today report no evidence of Chinese activity en route."

"What about the reconnaissance team COL MacLean sent out last night, sir?" Nick asked.

"Haven't heard anything," Faith said.

A sense of foreboding spread throughout the room like dark clouds before a violent storm. What happened to MacLean's reconnaissance team? They should've reported back long ago.

Wham. Crack. The sound of scattered rifle fire erupted along the perimeter. Someone doused the lantern.

"Those damn ROKs are too jumpy," Faith said. "Someone get them to calm down."

Nick rushed outside into the moonless night. Single rifle shots were coming from several locations flanking the defensive perimeter. Then the steady *rat tat tat* of his unit's machine guns and Browning automatic rifles.

"Hold your fire!" Nick shouted. "They're trying to locate our positions!"

The men of 1/32 IN stopped firing and enemy shots faded away in the frigid night air. Heart pounding like a locomotive, Nick rushed to his platoon dug in on the east side of the road and joined SGT Miller,. Moving among the trenches, they exhorted the men to fix bayonets and conserve their ammunition until the enemy was clearly in sight.

A whistle, followed by a bugle call, sounded the charge as dozens of white-quilted soldiers sprinted out of the darkness yelling epithets in Mandarin and English. Firing burp guns and rifles, the Chinese rushed the right flank of Nick's platoon. Nick's mind flashed to the Japanese attacks on New Guinea. *American you die!* He raised his rifle, released the safety lever and began blazing away as more and more enemy emerged from the darkness.

The roar of weapons and enemy screams blended in cacophonous fury. Although several enemy soldiers succeeded in breaching the perimeter, they were soon killed in vicious, hand-to-hand combat and the attack subsided.

Crouching in a trench, Nick assessed the situation. About fifty Chinese lay dead on the frozen ground outside the line of defense. Three of his men had been killed and four wounded. But the platoon held pretty damn well. "How many do you think, Mike?" He asked SGT Miller.

"Seemed about company-size to me, Lieutenant," Miller said. "We should get ready for a second wave."

In the darkness north of the road block an engine turned over, coughed, then roared to life. "Tank!" SGT Miller yelled moments before a Soviet-made, T-34 tank came rumbling around a curve in the icy road.

Nick ran to his recoilless rifle team entrenched behind sandbags east of the road. "Easy boys. Wait until he's well around the curve."

300 feet from the barricade, the tank fired a single shot from its powerful 76 mm gun. Fragments of wood, dust and ice flew up in the air like a flaming curtain. Before the T-34 could get off another shot, the recoilless rifle team raked its vulnerable turret with 75 mm fire. The tank lurched forward like a wounded rhino until more shots to its tracks sent it tumbling off the road into the ravine.

As mixed weapon fire erupted from the ridge east of the road, Able company's commander CPT Steward vaulted over the sandbags into Nick's trench. "They're going for our machine gun post on the high ground!" Steward yelled. "Let's get a rifle squad over there."

With CPT Steward in the lead, Nick and ten riflemen approached the ridge that was now eerily silent. Picking their way through a dozen, dead Chinese lying in the crimson-tinted snow, they cautiously climbed the hill. *Rat tat tat tat.* Halfway to the top, they were met with withering fire from two concealed machine gun positions. CPT Steward and three riflemen went down. Nick and the seven surviving men of the squad scrambled back down to their defensive positions on lower ground.

Throughout the night, the Chinese attacked various positions of 1/32 IN. Several enemy soldiers, skirting the perimeter, overran a mortar battery; but it was soon recaptured. Despite support from machine guns and automatic rifles, repeated attempts to recapture the ridge were unsuccessful. At first light, the enemy along the road had vanished like nocturnal, *mogwai* demons blending back into their snowy retreats in the mountainous terrain.

November 28, 1950

In the early morning, Faith's headquarters received a faint radio signal distorted by atmospheric interference. 3/31 IN reported an ongoing attack against their positions along the inlet south of 1/32 IN. Apparently the battalion's commander had been seriously wounded and a field artillery battery overrun by the Chinese. No communication was established with 1/31 IN or the 31st Tank company south of Hill 1221.

The 1/32 IN aid station, set up in a dilapidated, two-room farmhouse, was overflowing with 100 wounded when Nick went to check on one of his men. Twenty frozen bodies, wrapped in tarps, lined the crumbling outer wall of the abandoned, peasant home. The most seriously injured men lay on makeshift cots inside the farmhouse. Walking wounded, wrapped like mummies in bloody bandages, were huddled around camp stoves outside. But Nick was relieved. His rifleman had a clean bullet wound through his thigh. Although a bit gimpy, he could still shoulder his rifle.

Nick was dead tired. With three men killed in the unsuccessful assault on the ridge, his platoon was now down to fifteen fit and four walking wounded. His men had fought well. He was proud of them. But certainly there would be another Chinese attack tonight.

At 1400 X Corps Commander Lieutenant General Edward Almond arrived by helicopter at the 3/31 IN forward command post to meet with COL MacLean and his officers. A combat veteran of both world wars, LTG Almond had been appointed by General MacArthur to command UN forces during the Incheon landing in September. Now in charge of all UN forces in northeastern Korea, Almond was known for his impatience and demanding nature. With little concern for conventional military doctrine, Almond deployed his troops in regimental or battalion-sized task forces and sent them on independent missions without the benefit of mutual support. Almond demanded quick results. Often appearing on the front lines, he sought to demonstrate the courage he expected of his men.

Early in the meeting Nick realized that LTG Almond was only partially aware of the debacle that occurred the night before—and COL MacLean was not helping.

"It looks like you've been facing a few stragglers from the Chinese units west of the reservoir," Almond said. "Are you set to attack tomorrow morning, Allan?"

"We're in pretty good shape, General," COL MacLean said. "As soon as my 2nd Infantry Battalion and the 31st Tank Company get here, we're ready to attack north."

In pretty good shape? Jesus Christ. Nick couldn't believe his ears. *After losing all those men and officers last night! What is it with MacLean? We're freezing our asses off up here. Running low on ammunition with the PLA in the high ground all around us.*

Luckily, LTC Faith seemed to be asking some of the right questions. "I have some concerns, General," LTC Faith said. "Several POWs claimed they belonged to two entirely different PLA divisions."

LTG Almond kicked a chunk of snow with his boot tip. "Dammit, man! There aren't two Chinese divisions in all of Korea." He laid a heavy hand on Faith's shoulder. "Don't let a bunch of Chinese laundrymen fleeing north stop you!"

Almond shifted to a more paternalistic tone, no doubt intended to be inspirational. "Your battalion did a great job last night, Don. I have three silver stars I want to award to you and two men you select for bravery."

"All of my soldiers have been brave in combat, General," Faith said. He ordered the two, closest enlisted men to line up by his side—his jeep driver and a random rifleman. "Please award the medals to these men, General."

LTG Almond pinned the silver stars on Faith and his two men, then turned toward the semi circle of staff officers. "Remember, men. We're still attacking and we're going all the way to the Yalu. It's better to err on the side of audacity and momentum than on the side of caution."

Faith and MacLean accompanied LTG Almond to his helicopter. Then, with a few words that Nick couldn't hear over the slapping thrum of the helicopter's blades, Almond pointed dramatically in a northern direction before climbing aboard the chopper to fly back to the Marine base at the southern tip of the reservoir.

COL MacLean returned to his Jeep. "I'll be at my headquarters," he told LTC Faith. "The tanks and Second

Infantry Battalion should arrive this afternoon. Be ready to shove off at dawn."

The moment the jeep was out of sight, Faith tore the Silver Star from his lapel and flung it into a snowbank.

"What did General Almond say?" Nick asked.

"You heard him," Faith said bitterly. "We're mounting an attack on a group of Chinese laundry men who are just trying to get back north."

At 1500, while making rounds with LTC Faith, Nick was startled to see COL MacLean's jeep return to the southern perimeter of 1/32 IN. "There's a Chinese roadblock at the inlet," MacLean told Faith. "Looks like I'll have to stay here tonight. I'm not sure when 2/31 and the tanks will move up, but we should be able to bust through the roadblock easily in the morning."

Nick flashed a sidelong glance at SGT Miller. The Chinese were surrounding RCT-31. Communications were down and it didn't look like the 31st Tank Company or the 2/31 Infantry Battalion would be arriving soon. When would COL MacLean realize that we're all alone up here?

Shortly before dark, Navy Corsairs radioed CPT Stamford that they'd strafed a battalion-size, PLA unit heading south on the reservoir road. Although the attack inflicted many casualties, an undetermined number of PLA were now scattered several miles north of 1/32 IN's perimeter.

At 2000 the terrain between the mountains and the reservoir was unusually quiet as Nick and SGT Miller walked along the east side of the road where their riflemen were dug into frozen, muddy snowbanks or lying on tarps behind the machine gun and recoilless rifle teams. Tonight there had been none of the usual enemy probes where PLA scouts tried to draw fire from 1/32 IN's automatic weapons to determine their exact positions.

Nick allowed a glimmer of hope to cross his mind. Maybe the Chinese were backing off? They'd had pretty heavy losses. And a task force could be on its way north to help us fight our way out. Nick didn't know. But he sure as hell knew his battalion had to make it to the Marines at Hagaru-ri. Were the Chinese really leaving? Or were they just waiting for the opportunity to annihilate both the Marines and RCT-31? Who the hell knew?

Wrapped in blankets, Nick and SGT Miller huddled behind a heavy, log barricade laid across the north end of the road and fired up a portable gas stove to heat some water for coffee. "How about some B unit rations?" SGT Miller said, opening a box containing three pieces of chocolate fudge, three biscuits, three pressed sugar cubes and a small tin of instant coffee. "Looks like everyone on watch is awake," Miller said. "But the men are pretty edgy."

"I know, Mike. Our platoon's not as tight as I'd like it to be. It's bad enough when an occasional ROK bugs out."

"Too bad we lost LT Lee," SGT Miller said. "He kept those ROKs pretty much in line. They fought a helluva lot better than I expected."

"What about our guys, Mike?"

"They're cold and hungry, Lieutenant. And pretty worried since COL MacLean couldn't get back down the road this afternoon."

"Goddamnit! It looks like the PLA is all around us, Mike. And the only communication we have is through Stamford's

245

Corsair pilots. With our bullshit intel, it's anyone's guess how many Chinese are out there."

"General Almond seems to think we're still on the offensive," Miller said. "To me, it looks the other way around." He took a slug of lukewarm coffee. "But our guys can still fight, Lieutenant. If they don't freeze to death first."

Chapter Twenty Six
Kanggye

WASHINGTON—*Top US diplomatic officials said Friday that developments in the next four or five days should decide whether the United States goes to war with Communist China...At the same time, the officials applauded Gen. MacArthur's all out offensive to end the Korean fighting by Christmas, and pointed out that he has authority to "clean out" Korea.*

Nippon Times

November 26, 1950

NKPA Military Hospital

Kanggye, DPRK

November 26, 1950

When they finally completed their hospital rounds in the late evening, the exhausted Ho-jun and Dr. Zhang returned to the deserted doctors lounge on the top floor of the hospital. Ho-jun began roasting some buckwheat kernels on a one-burner, gas stove atop a counter pockmarked with old burns.

"I know it's supposed to be good for blood circulation, Ho-jun," Dr. Zhang said. "But buckwheat tea is a little heavy for me and has a slight musky scent."

Ho-jun laughed. "I imagine you prefer Manchurian Mushroom tea, Comrade Teacher."

"No. *Kombucha* tea's not for me. I like good, black tea from Anhui province."

"I guess we're not so different. We each bring a part of our culture along with us."

"We work well together, Ho-jun. I'm proud of what a fine physician you've become."

"Thank you, Comrade Teacher. You prepared me well."

Although UN forces were still advancing, Ho-jun was breathing more easily now. When the Chinese PLA crossed over the Yalu, a new war had begun in Korea.

Now, undetected by UN intelligence services, thousands of PLA soldiers were crossing south over the Yalu. Like rugged Siberian tigers, they crept undetected into the frigid, mountains of the DPRK.

Eager to be home by Christmas, isolated UN regiments and battalions were thrusting north around the Changjin reservoir unaware they were driving into the center of a well-planned attack by an overwhelming PLA force.

Known euphemistically as the People's *Volunteer* Army in Korea, many of its soldiers were seasoned, combat veterans of the struggle against Imperial Japan and the civil war against the Nationalist Chinese. Like ancient Chinese warriors facing chariot-borne, Aryan invaders, PLA soldiers were innovative and resilient when faced with a modern, mechanized enemy.

When their teas were well-brewed, Ho-jun and Dr. Zhang sat down at a pine-topped, kitchen table. "Since you arrived here," Ho-jun said, "I've noticed some differences between our soldiers. Your men seem happier."

"Our system is more egalitarian than yours, Ho-jun. We have no ranks below General. We recruit PLA units with men from the same area or province. They care about one another. They fight fiercely in small units. They're encouraged to discuss and problem solve military issues. Many military leaders are promoted from the ranks."

"I'm impressed, Comrade Teacher. Your military system is quite different from ours. We follow the model of our Soviet teachers."

Dr. Zhang nodded respectfully. "We follow the guerrilla tactics of Mao. Our attack forces sweep around enemy flanks, looking for a weak spot to penetrate with overwhelming force. Then we cut off the rear from reinforcement or retreat and close around the enemy like a tightening vice."

Ho-jun looked out the frosted window at the dim lights flickering in the darkness of the devastated city. A bitter sadness spread throughout his chest. American bombing had been indiscriminate. Many more civilians than military personnel had been injured or killed. Survivors living in thatched tents or makeshift shelters fashioned from salvaged rubble and timber were now at risk for death by exposure to the extreme cold.

"Do you think your Chinese air force can challenge US air power, Comrade Teacher?"

"Not yet, Ho-jun."

"Yesterday on rounds you mentioned a rumor about action at the Changjin Reservoir, Comrade Teacher. Can you tell me more?"

Dr. Zhang paused and looked around the empty doctors lounge. "It's not just a rumor, Ho-jun," he said in a lowered voice. "We have 120,000 men in the mountains waiting for the bugle call to attack 30,000 American troops who are strung out along the reservoir. The enemy is confident but less than vigilant. He's been told the war is almost over. The ROK units are notoriously unreliable in the face of an attack. And the Yankees are daylight distance fighters. They're not used to hand-to-hand fighting. Our PLA will attack at night with superior force."

Narrowing his eyes, Dr, Zhang focused his gaze on Ho-jun. "At the request of the PLA Medical Corps, you're being assigned with me to a field hospital near the reservoir. I suspect we're going to have a lot of casualties, Ho-jun."

Ho-jun felt a vague, fluttering sensation in his stomach. "Where is this field hospital, Comrade Teacher?"

"On the forested, western slope of the mountains. About eight kilometers from the battle zone."

"Is there anything there now?"

"Only a small rifle squad and an aide station. But a PLA construction unit has been busy preparing the site to accommodate more casualties."

November 27, 1950

At 0600 with SGT Hak at the wheel, Ho-jun headed deep into the forested, western slope of the snow-covered Taebaek Mountains. Close behind the jeep, three cargo trucks and two ambulances carried his team of NKPA medical corpsmen and driver/aides. A few kilometers ahead, Dr. Zhang's PLA medical team was already out of sight.

Ho-jun was impressed when they arrived at the newly constructed field hospital in mid-afternoon. Most of the

Chinese troops preparing the site were former farmers, skilled in construction and camouflage. A semi-circular, corrugated steel, Quonset hut had been wedged into a cavity carved into the hillside and lined with canvas cots for triage. A heated log cabin, its roof covered with evergreen brush and snow, was assembled as the patient ward. Numerous tents and tarpaulins, layered with snow, had been stretched between the trees to hide vehicles, personnel and supplies from the air.

Stomping their boots on the sturdy, wooden staircase, Ho-jun and SGT Hak entered the log cabin and stripped off their winter parkas. Dr. Zhang and a PLA corpsman were already making rounds on the first few patients who had been transported from the combat zone around the Changjin Reservoir.

"The aide stations close to the battle zone will still be handling frostbite and minor injuries," Dr. Zhang said. "They have warming tents and basic medical supplies. We'll only get the seriously wounded here."

Speaking Mandarin, Ho-jun and Dr. Zhang proceeded to evaluate the wounded PLA soldiers together. Although SGT Hak readily grasped the condition of most patients, Ho-jun occasionally paused to clarify an issue for him in Korean. The majority of battle injuries were from small arms fire, hand grenades or mortars. A few were from face-to-face fighting with knives and bayonets.

As the patient volume grew, Ho-jun and Dr. Zhang split into PLA and DPRK teams. As usual, Ho-jun felt supported by the excellent SGT Hak who led their medical squad in four, well-organized teams. Most of the cases were familiar to Ho-jun's corpsmen—bullet wounds, shrapnel, shock, lacerations and fractures. Occasionally Ho-jun consulted his mentor Dr. Zhang regarding a complicated case.

At 2200 Ho-jun and Dr. Zhang sat by a stove beneath the snow-covered opening of the quonset hut. The air was so cold that, despite the stove, Ho-jun's fingers stuck to the steel sides of the cup holding his freshly brewed tea, now layered with a thin film of ice. Dr. Zhang lit two *Chunghwa* cigarettes and handed one to Ho-jun. "What do you think of these?" He asked, tapping the bright red package, emblazoned with golden images of the Tiananmen gate and Huabiao pillars. "It's Chairman Mao's favorite. Our national cigarette."

Ho-jun exhaled a stream of smoke that slowly dissipated in the Arctic air. "Tastes a bit like plums, don't you think, Comrade Teacher? But I must admit they're better than the cigarettes I've been rolling with strips of the *Rodong Sinmun.*"

"We should get some rest while we can," Dr. Zhang said. "The attack at the reservoir is scheduled for tonight. Once our men are committed by the call of a bugle or a whistle, there's no turning back. Although this tactic usually works against the weakest point of the enemy line, it also results in a lot of PLA casualties." Dr. Zhang's expression darkened like the sky before a tornado. "I suspect we'll get a significant influx of patients before morning, Ho-jun. But I guess that's the secret to our military success. We're willing to sacrifice large numbers of brave men to achieve victory."

November 28, 1950

At 0400, wedged in a corner of the log cabin beneath three army blankets, Ho-jun was awakened by SGT Hak's tug on his shoulder. "You need to get up, Comrade Doctor. There are lots of wounded coming in."

Ho-jun rapidly cleared his head of sleep when he saw the exhausted, litter bearers and the bloody splints and bandages of the seriously wounded men streaming into the log cabin. Joining SGT Hak, he began rapid triage of the patients cared for by his four teams of corpsmen: Major hemorrhage. Airway obstruction. Poor respiration. Poor circulation. Hypothermia. Shock. Any one of these indicated level I, the most dangerously wounded.

"His systolic blood pressure by palpation is 80. Pulse 90 and faint, Comrade Doctor." An NKPA corpsman caring for a comatose, PLA soldier reported. "He has massive wounds of the chest and abdomen. He received two bags of plasma and 10 mg. of morphine twice while en route by stretcher. His breathing is becoming slow and erratic."

SGT Hak lifted one corner of the bulky dressing. Much of the anterior wall of the chest and abdomen had been blown away. "Probably a mortar," he said, looking up at Ho-jun.

Ho-jun nodded and turned to the young corpsman. "There is nothing we can do. Just keep him as comfortable as possible." He started to move on, then turned briefly. "And increase the morphine dose to 40 mg as needed."

By mid-afternoon the steady flow of seriously wounded soldiers into the field hospital began to slow down. But corpsmen reported that far more PLA soldiers lay dead and frozen on the perimeter of the battlefield. This was the predictable result of the tactics Dr. Zhang had described. During an attack, PLA soldiers fell to the ground as enemy fire increased. Once there was a relative lull, they rose to continue the attack. With each surge more PLA soldiers were killed, but with an unending stream of reinforcements, the attack continued until they were all annihilated or able to break through the line.

Ho-jun was preparing to take a brief rest when he noticed that a female PLA corpsman was evaluating a new admission. Although the patient's back was turned, the two silver diamonds and oak cluster on his blood-soaked epaulets identified him as an ROK 1st Lieutenant. Perhaps he'd been transported to the hospital for interrogation.

Just as he was about to exit the log cabin, Ho-jun felt the urge to turn around. There was something familiar about the wounded ROK officer. As he strode toward the man, now lying listless and supine on a floor mat, Ho-jun's breath came up short. The long, jagged scar spreading across his left cheek was unmistakable. Kwang-min!

"I know this man," Ho-jun said to the startled Chinese corpsman. "What's his condition?"

"He's had multiple bullet wounds to the upper body, Comrade Doctor," the corpsman said. She turned Ho-jun aside. "He was initially lucid, but now appears to be moribund. Dr. Zhang told us to keep him comfortable. I've just given him 10 mg. of morphine."

Ho-jun thanked the corpsman and knelt beside Kwang-min who was clearly dying. The world spun around in his mind. The last time he'd seen Kwang-min he was in the Imperial Japanese Army. Now he wore the uniform of a lieutenant in the ROK Army. "Kwang-min. It's Ho-jun," he said softly.

Kwang-min's eyes slowly opened. Squinting into Ho-jun's face, he managed a weak, half-smile, then lapsed into unconsciousness.

Ho-jun placed a hand on the shoulder of his old childhood friend. The boy he'd raced up the steep steps of their Pyongyang neighborhood. The high school teammate who'd shovel-passed him the final shot in the Korean high school basketball finals. The boy who'd always dreamed of attending the Imperial Japanese Military Academy in Mukden.

Kwang-min's face slowly turned ashen, and his breathing transitioned into a series of brief gasps. Then with a sudden jerk of his shoulders, the muscles of his face relaxed and he was still. Ho-jun remained by his side for a few more minutes, then headed outside.

Soft snowflakes cascading down from the slate-gray sky dissolved in the tears welling up in his eyes as Ho-jun walked aimlessly into the forest. With a sudden flutter of its wings, a scarlet bird darted between the snow-laden branches of a tall pine tree. *We're just a flash of lightning in a summer cloud. A bubble in a stream. This world will pass like a star at dawn.*

Chapter Twenty Seven
Arctic Fire

REDS UNLEASH NEW ATTACKS—*Chinese and North Korean Communists hurled new attacks against the center of the United Nations lines in northwest Korea Monday, but they faced trouble from the east as US Marines drove westward from the Chosin reservoir area toward the enemy's exposed rear.*

Nippon Times
November 28, 1950

Chosin Reservoir
November 29, 1950

Shortly after midnight the landscape north of the Pungnyuri inlet was bathed in pale moonlight when Nick and Sergeant Miller made their rounds along the northern perimeter of 1/32 IN. Wrapped in grim silence, the men of Nick's platoon awaited the next Chinese attack. Some, aware that the Chinese had bayoneted sleeping GIs in their foxholes, stood with their sleeping bags pulled up to their waists and arms wrapped around their weapons. Others clapped their hands and paced about to keep their legs moving in the merciless cold.

At 30 degrees F below zero, truck batteries went dead and their fuel pumps froze. Several trucks ran all night in order to jumpstart the others in the morning. Ammunition, food and gasoline were running low. Completely out of sterile bandages, the corpsmen and had only a few remaining morphine syrettes which they held in their mouth to keep from freezing.

The midnight silence was broken only by periodic firing of American weapons to keep them from jamming with frost-lock. Huddled together in their foxholes like Siberian chipmunks, the men of Nick's rifle platoon were exhausted, awaiting the next Chinese attack. Many of the men had early signs of frostbite—fingers, noses and toes turning red and cold to the touch. A few with blood blisters, blue fingers and toes had been placed in the medical warming tent.

Swaddled against their bodies beneath multiple layers of clothing, the men defrosted C-rations and protected weapons that could be damaged by the cold—grenades, gun barrels, pistols and ammunition.

Crunch. Each step Nick took into the crusty snow required a great effort to withdraw. He'd never been in such extreme cold. Not even in the highest Cascades. It sapped his energy and slowed him down. Despite multiple layers of clothing, Nick could not escape the numbing effect of the Arctic wind along the shore of the Chosin Reservoir. Without frequent movement, rubbing and stretching, his legs felt like frozen logs, his trigger finger stiff as an icy twig.

There was occasional small arms fire, but no major Chinese attacks throughout the night. At 0630, one hour before sunrise, Nick's forward rifle company began moving south toward the inlet to join with 3/31 IN. Recognizing the American withdrawal, the PLA increased its rifle, mortar and machine gun fire—then backed off to sporadic rifle shots that faded into the morning light like lonely cries of the long-winged *Nightjar*.

At daybreak, the I,32 IN convoy was moving south without significant opposition. Walking with his platoon along the high ground east of the road, Nick's pace became steady and focused—he was beginning to feel optimistic about the breakout. Chinese activity had definitely decreased. Maybe Almond was right. The PLA *could* be pulling out. For the first time in days, Nick allowed his mind to drift into a reverie. The morning call of crows high in the cherry trees of Tokyo's Yoyogi Park. Ruth lying close to him in bed...*Hold it!*

Nick's platoon froze at a bend in the road. The point man, 200 feet ahead, was kneeling with one arm raised. Nick climbed to higher ground to scan the area with his binoculars. The road along the reservoir's shoreline was turning northeast to circle a long finger of ice. At the end of the narrow gravel strip was a Chinese roadblock of large boulders and logs. Less than a mile beyond the roadblock, Nick could see small arms fire flashing back-and-forth along the friendly perimeter of 3/31 IN.

With two heavy machine guns and a recoilless rifle nested on the high ground above the road, the riflemen of Able and Charlie Companies circled behind the roadblock from the east. Crouching against the rugged, ridge line 150 feet above the reservoir, Nick could see that most of the PLA force was engaged in a full-scale assault on 3/31 IN. Nevertheless, the roadblock 1,500 feet ahead, was manned with two heavy

261

machine guns and a platoon of infantrymen armed with Russian *burp* guns and stick hand grenades.

"I don't think they've seen us yet, Lieutenant," Miller said.

"Doesn't look like it. But their communications are even worse than ours."

"Bugles and whistles are better than nothing when your com lines are out, Lieutenant."

Nick and SGT Miller leaned into the crusty snow of the ridgeline and tried to cover their ears with frozen gloves. Moments later, 1/32 IN's heavy machine gun and recoilless rifle teams belched devastating, red tracer fire on the PLA roadblock below. Green Chinese tracers briefly flew back up toward the ridge. Then, with smoke and flames engulfing the roadblock, all machine gun fire ceased. The PLA infantry platoon, outnumbered, with no machine gun support, was retreating into the hills.

A dense, curtain of smoke drifted across the road when RCT-31's heavy weapons finally ceased firing. Time seemed to slow down as Nick advanced cautiously toward the fallen PLA roadblock. The machine gun positions were smoldering ruins, their crews strewn in red-tinged snow. And, like phantoms exuded from a dark cloud of destruction, PLA infantrymen were slipping into the hills. Slowly at first, then desperately, they scrambled toward the snow-covered forest as half-hearted, American small arms fire raked their retreat.

Nick didn't like shooting at fleeing, enemy soldiers. No one really did. It seemed somehow dishonorable. He nodded *enough* to Sergeant Miller. "Hold your fire! Save your ammo!" SGT Miller bellowed.

Nick's platoon charged downhill toward the now-abandoned PLA roadblock. Scrambling over the bodies of their comrades lying dead along the slope, scattered groups of PLA were disappearing into the forest. When all firing ceased, a growling half-track bulldozed the roadblock's large branches and boulders downslope into the reservoir. The convoy then resumed slowly down the road.

Like a shaft of sunlight breaking through wintry clouds, a powerful influx of energy coursed through Nick's body. The PLA was on the run. His platoon had performed well. Maybe they'd still get out of this.

With COL MacLean riding like a pharaoh in the lead jeep, the convoy was approaching the perimeter of 3/31 IN when a sudden burst of fire erupted from the 3/31's southeast perimeter. Before anyone could stop him, COL MacLean bolted from the jeep and rushed down the reservoir road, waving his arms and shouting: "Don't fire! That's 2/31! They're our boys!"

The first burst of PLA gunfire knocked MacLean to his knees, but he rose and stumbled forward a few more steps before three more bursts took him down and several PLA riflemen dragged his limp body into the brush.

Bellowing the Army battle cry *hooah!* LTC Faith led a skirmish line directly across the ice to attack the PLA unit that was besieging the perimeter of 3/31 IN. Sandwiched between two enemy forces, dozens of the attacking PLA soldiers were killed before the rest of them faded into the forested hills east of the reservoir. When the smoke cleared, many PLA bodies lay scattered like fallen leaves across the frozen battle ground.

Some bore American weapons, others wore US Army boots or field jackets.

LTC Faith assumed command of both infantry battalions. After a brief meeting with his officers, he organized a narrow perimeter on the low, sloping ground between several abandoned Korean houses and a railroad track running along the reservoir. With clear skies, air support could resupply and protect their current position. If reinforcements didn't arrive soon, the plan was to regroup and continue moving south.

Unfortunately, with supplies running dangerously low, one C-47 air drop of ammunition and food in the afternoon went to the enemy. But two others were successfully retrieved.

Throughout the day and moonlit-night, gull-winged Navy Corsairs napalmed, rocketed and strafed PLA forces on the high ground surrounding RCT-31. At 0100 a Corsair pilot radioed the air controller CPT Stamford with disturbing news. *There are so many PLA in the area, I can drop my bombs just about anywhere.*

November 30, 1950

Except for a few, small probes, there were no PLA attacks during the night. At daylight, Navy Corsairs reappeared to sweep over the high ground like bent-wing eagles searching for PLA troops threatening RCT-31. But there was no sign of enemy soldiers. They were either well-camouflaged or had withdrawn from the area. Slowly, with increasing confidence, the men of RCT-31 began to move about. Small fires, built to warm frozen hands and feet, drew no PLA fire. Spirits rose. *Maybe they had withstood the worst? Surely a relief column would arrive from the south today.*

In the late afternoon a litter-bearing helicopter made two uncontested landings in a clearing west of Hill 1221 to evacuate several seriously wounded soldiers. Darkness fell with no sign of the enemy. While the men of their platoon cleaned their weapons and sharpened their bayonets, Nick and SGT Miller huddled behind a half-track to heat some C rations.

"Just like Mama used to make," Miller said as he dipped his hardtack biscuit into a can of corned beef.

"I thought New Mexicans ate only chili and tamales."

"Yeah. Just like you Northwesters only eat salmon."

"What do you think's up, Mike?" Nick said. "The Chinese are pretty quiet."

"I don't know, Lieutenant. Could be they're backing off, but I wouldn't count on it."

"You know. Compared to the Japs on New Guinea? They don't seem so fanatical to me."

"Yeah, maybe. But Chinese attacks sure are full bore. They keep charging at our soft spots until they can break through. They lose a lot of men that way."

At 2200, a red flare rose above the high ground to the east. Then, with a whistle blast, a company-sized unit of PLA charged the perimeter of RCT-31. With clanging cymbals and bugle calls, the Chinese infantrymen shrieked something that, to Nick, sounded like "*you die!*"

Brilliant white light scintillated from parachuting star shells as red and green tracers arced back and forth over the frozen hillside. White-quilted soldiers, firing burp guns and flinging fragmentation hand grenades, rushed into the perimeter of Able Company.

Crouching behind the log barrier, Nick fired his rifle as fast as he could. But the PLA kept charging—farmers and peasants leaping like Kung Fu fighters over the bodies of their comrades. They were almost on top of Nick. Was this the end?

Then about 300 feet out, everything changed as four heavy machine guns mounted on an antiaircraft half-track drew a curtain of death back and forth across the charging PLA infantrymen. Ten men. A dozen. More than a hundred dead PLA lay stacked one over another across the icy, gravel road.

At 2300 a gently hissing snow was beginning to blanket the PLA dead lying on the road as Nick and SGT Miller silently walked the perimeter of their defensive positions. Miller briefly removed a glove and fished in his pockets. "Try this," he said. "It came with the last airdrop." He handed Nick a frozen Tootsie Roll.

Nick and SGT Miller walked through their platoon checking each foxhole to be sure one man was awake. They examined the placement of machine gun, recoilless rifle and mortar positions. They asked the men how they were maintaining their weapons in the extreme cold. Sometimes they'd engage in brief banter. But mostly they kept moving together like parts of a well-oiled, fighting machine. Both seasoned veterans of the Pacific War, Nick and SGT Miller were a good team.

After midnight, small PLA units repeatedly hurled themselves against the perimeter, but counterattacks by Nick's Able Company drove them back to the high ground. At dawn, the PLA made one final, concerted attack, but withdrew after withering fire from RCT-31's heavy machine guns and recoilless rifles slashed into their screaming onslaught, felling dozens.

Chapter Twenty Eight
Desperation

WASHINGTON (AP)—Text of President Truman's statement today: *The Chinese Communist leaders have sent their troops from Manchuria to launch a strong and well organized attack against the United Nations forces in North Korea...resulting in the forced withdrawal of large parts of the United Nations command. The battlefield situation is uncertain at this time.*

New York Times
November 30, 1950

Chosin Reservoir
December 1, 1950

Under overcast skies, Nick went to the medical unit to check on two of his riflemen. The treatment tent was filled to capacity and dozens of wounded men lay beneath tarpaulins on litters improvised from ponchos and field jackets. Those able to drink, sipped coffee and hot soup heated over a field stove. With no sterile bandages, the medics wrapped wounds in any reasonably clean fabric they could find—strips of underwear, towels and parachutes. Reserving the dwindling supply of morphine for the most severe cases, aspirin was the only pain medicine readily available.

"How are you doing, Matthews?" Nick asked a towheaded rifleman from Idaho whose shoulder was wrapped like a blood-stained piñata in a strip torn from a red and white parachute salvaged from an ammunition drop.

"Not so bad, Lieutenant," the young man said through half-clenched teeth. "But ain't this bonkers?" He gestured with his good arm toward his thickly wrapped toes. "The frostbite was bad enough."

The second rifleman from Nick's platoon, a seasoned corporal from Seattle, was only semi-conscious with his head and neck wrapped in multiple bandages. As Nick laid a silent hand on his shoulder, a passing medic whispered. "Bullet to the neck and grenade fragments to the head. I just gave him some morphine. Not much more we can do, sir."

At noon, Nick and SGT Miller huddled around a small fire eating cans of frozen beans and vegetable stew mixed with ice crystals. *Thud!* A pressurized heat wave swept across their bodies. *Wham!* The explosion of a nearby mortar shell was followed by the strange, buzzing sound of shrapnel fragments swarming like bees through the air.

Nick and Miller scampered to relative safety beneath the tailgate of a 2 1/2 ton truck. "That mother was close," SGT Miller said. "But it still didn't have my number. Sometimes I feel like I'm 1,000 years old."

Shortly before noon, LTC Faith met with the RCT-31 officers. "Captain Stamford just received a message from a Corsair pilot flying over our position." Faith said. "If the weather clears, more Corsairs will arrive this afternoon." Faith paused. "But the pilot also told us there were no *friendlies* coming up the road." He looked around the circle of battle-weary officers. "Looks like we're on our own, boys. If the skies clear, we'll break out this afternoon with a single push to Hagaru-ri."

In preparation for the breakout, 22 intact, 2-1/2-ton trucks were filled with gasoline siphoned from severely damaged vehicles. Wooden pallets were layered across the truck beds to accommodate two levels of stretchers for wounded men. Artillery and mortar men were ordered to expend all their ammunition and destroy their weapons with white phosphorus and thermite grenades. Anti-aircraft halftracks were designated to protect the front and rear, and jeeps, mounted with machine guns, were interspersed throughout the column.

At 1300, with Corsairs crisscrossing a clear sky, RCT-31 loaded the wounded into trucks and began moving south with 1/32 riflemen walking along the high ground to protect the vehicles. The 3/31 IN Battalion, badly battered by the Chinese the night before, limped along, guarding the rear.

Navy Corsairs roared low overhead, strafing and dropping napalm on PLA troops on the high ground and those coming up the road from the south. Although their losses were heavy, Chinese attacks did not abate. Under continuous fire, RCT-31 crawled along the gravel road for two miles before disaster struck.

A Corsair, releasing its napalm canisters too soon, spewed a blazing carpet of jellied gasoline across the squad walking the lead. Several men were incinerated immediately. Others, coated with gelatinous flames, screamed and beat their arms against their blazing uniforms as they stumbled about like flaming zombies or rolled in the banks of crusty snow lining the road.

Like a fiery wind, a sense of panic swept through the ranks of infantrymen walking the road. With so many casualties, there were few able-bodied officers and senior noncoms available to hold the line. Tactical control began to unravel as men left their security positions along the high ground and raced on down the road.

Nick and SGT Miller organized a ten-man squad to advance rapidly ahead of the slowly moving column. After a mile, they came upon three, fire-blackened American tanks that had been abandoned by the roadside with their treads and turrets ajar. Several Chinese soldiers were clambering over the destroyed vehicles, stripping anything useful they could find.

Kill! Goddam Chinks! Nick and his men screamed obscenities as they ran firing their weapons toward the startled Chinese. Several PLA soldiers fell dead; the rest scattered. Nick spat on the ground and turned to SGT Miller. "So much for the tanks coming to our rescue. They never even made it to Hill 1221."

Two miles from their starting point, the convoy was stopped by a blown bridge and machine gun fire coming from the high ground. While Nick's platoon returned the intense fire from above, a halftrack towed the trucks filled with wounded men across the shallow stream. Although Chinese bullets pinged off their metal surfaces and pierced their canvas canopies, most of the trucks made it safely to the other side.

But one truck, stuck in the middle of the stream, was riddled with intense, Chinese fire. Despite the efforts of the mighty halftrack and a dozen men straining like oxen to prevent it from tipping over, the truck burst into flames and wounded men fell screaming into the icy water. Survivors were loaded into intact trucks and by late afternoon, the last truck had crossed the stream.

At twilight, the convoy encountered another PLA roadblock at a hairpin turn. As its twin machine guns poured fire into the barrier, the lead halftrack was struck with rocket-propelled missiles from a captured American bazooka. Rear treads unraveled and the smoking vehicle careened across the road, raked by heavy, Chinese machine gun fire. The driver and two men manning the rear-mounted machine guns were killed.

The convoy idled 300 feet from the roadblock as LTC Faith paced back and-forth like a snow leopard contemplating his next move. Each time he passed his Jeep he squeezed off a round of .50 caliber fire from the machine gun mounted in the rear. "Jackson!" He yelled to Nick. "You take the high ground south of the barricade. I'll lead an assault team from the north."

With rifles and hand grenades, Nick's platoon destroyed a machine gun nest perched above the roadblock, then circled around and attacked the PLA infantrymen behind the barrier. Simultaneously, shouting *hooah!* LTC Faith led a dozen men in a charge directly at the roadblock. Shortly before his team overran the remaining Chinese infantrymen, a potato masher hand grenade skipped over the frozen road and detonated a few feet from Faith.

Mortally wounded, Faith was placed in the cab of a truck and the convoy moved on. At twilight, a flight of four Corsairs flew overhead attempting to strafe PLA positions in front of RCT-31's column. But once again friendly fire proved deadly —in the fading light, several men walking in front of the trucks were hit. Just as the sun went down, LTC Faith died.

A number of men, feeling retreat on the road was doomed, began slipping away from the convoy. Although Nick and SGT Miller managed to hold their platoon together, discipline was unraveling quickly and some men began to race wildly down the road ahead of the trucks. Nick saw the futility of trying to stop terrified men from leaving the convoy. Where would they go? Right into the arms of PLA coming up the road? Down the steep slope toward the reservoir where they would be easy targets? Up to the high ground where the PLA was embedded? Nick kept trudging along. He did not want to leave trucks full of wounded men unguarded.

Snow began to blanket the road with icy, white crystals as RCT-31 moved south toward the small logging village of Hudong-ni. With no obvious Chinese opposition, riflemen along the road climbed onto running boards and hoods as the lead trucks picked up speed. Nick and SGT Miller hopped into a jeep in the middle of the column.

Nick held a gloved hand in front of his face to shield it from the wind-blown snowflakes melting into his eyes. Where would the PLA hit next? He looked up at the dark clouds sweeping across the waning moon. Only a few rounds left in his rifle's ammunition clip. Still about eight clicks to Hagaru-ri. And 1500 clicks to Ruth in Tokyo. Hank Williams' plaintive voice drifted through Nick's mind. *The moon just went behind the cloud to hide its face and cry.*

As Nick's jeep rumbled through the outskirts of Hudong-ni, steel-gray clouds swept across the-moon, casting shadows on stacks of snow-covered timber. Although dim light shined through the cracks of a small building on the hillside above the village, the sawmill, cabins and huts were all dark. Nick wasn't surprised. Many of the villages along the reservoir became deserted once the war came to them.

Whomp! A red ball of fire with an orange core shot up from the lead truck 300 feet ahead. Then *brat a tat tat.* Chinese heavy machine guns opened up. By following the green tracers back to their origin, Nick identified two PLA machine gun positions on a rooftop and in a wooden hut.

"How much ammo you got left?" Nick asked SGT Miller.

"Two eight round clips. One hand grenade. One rifle grenade."

"I've only got eight rounds left," Nick said.

"What do you think, Lieutenant? Try to take out the hut?"

Nick and SGT Miller gathered eight, able-bodied riflemen into a squad and sprinted toward the front of the column. The first three trucks of the convoy were ablaze and immobile in the middle of the road through the village. Drowning out the screams of wounded men trapped inside, heavy machine gun fire swept over the burning trucks.

Unable to advance, the fourth truck roared back-and-forth, charging into the rear of the flaming pile up ahead like a raging bull. Ducking low behind the wheel as bullets raked the body and shattered the windshield of his truck, the heroic driver finally succeeded in pushing the disabled vehicles to the side of the road. Under continuous PLA machine gun fire, the trucks began moving again.

Divided into two fire teams on either side of a narrow road that was rutted with frozen mud and snow, Nick's squad crept toward the bursts of machine gun fire erupting from the partially opened shutter of a weatherbeaten hut. In the lead 300 feet from the hut, SGT Miller lowered his left hand. *Down.*

Miller planted his left knee in the frozen ground and affixed a tube-shaped grenade launcher to the barrel of his rifle. He loaded a blank cartridge into the rifle's magazine and unhooked a rifle grenade from his belt. Attaching it to the launcher, he removed the grenade's pin, allowing the launcher's safety spoon to hold the grenade's strike lever in place until fired. With his right heel pressed against his buttocks, Miller hooked his left elbow around his right knee and raised the rifle into firing position.

Brrap-Pap-Pap-Pap. The rapid fire of a burp gun erupted 75 feet ahead as a squad of Chinese soldiers burst from a dark, side street. Riddled with bullets, SGT Miller and two of his fire team fell to the ground. With a racing pulse, Nick knelt and fired his rifle at the charging Chinese infantrymen until his clip ran out. Several PLA went down, but soon his team was engaged in hand-to-hand combat with seven enemy soldiers.

A stocky, Chinese soldier thrust his bayonet forward and simultaneously kicked at Nick's leg. Nick instantly recognized the maneuver. *Sanda*—a military variation of Kung Fu not unlike the jujitsu used by the Japanese on New Guinea. Nick spun sideways and caught the attacker's ankle sending him to the ground, then killed him with his rifle bayonet. Nick turned toward the four surviving men of his assault team who were battling six Chinese soldiers up close with fists and KA-bar knives. Nick jammed the last clip into his rifle's magazine and fired all eight rounds, killing four PLA. One more member of his team was killed before all the Chinese attackers were dead.

Nick picked up SGT Miller's M1, squatted low in the middle of the dark road and assumed firing position. Focusing on the red, PLA muzzle flash bursting through an opening in the hut's shutter, he aligned his right eye through the rifle's sights and relaxed his arms and shoulders. Grounding himself with two slow breaths in and out, he gently squeezed the trigger. *Blam*. The rifle grenade scored a direct hit. The PLA machine gun went silent as flames swept up the side of the cabin, igniting its thick, bark roof and pine siding. Nick knelt and gently touched SGT Miller's bloody forehead. *Jesus Mike. We only had a little ways to go.*

Chong a! Sha! A squad of Chinese soldiers shouting battle cries meaning charge! and kill! came rushing down the street toward Nick and the three surviving men of his team. Nick shouted "Retreat!" and began running down the road toward the convoy. Rapid, burp gun fire dropped two of the men running behind him. "Spread out!" Nick shouted just as his last squad member stumbled and fell dead to the ground. Nick ran on as fast as he could in the darkness. Pursuing PLA fire dwindled, then ceased when he approached the main road.

No trucks were moving through the village. Under continuous machine gun fire, they hadn't travelled far. Tires went flat. Radiators burst. Windshields were shattered. Trucks with dead drivers veered off the road. Some turned over. Others caught fire. The cries of wounded men trapped inside the burning trucks, merged with gunfire, shouts and explosions in a cacophony of pain, terror and destruction.

Nick fired the remainder of SGT Miller's clip at a squad of PLA soldiers running up the road like *Yaoguai* demons flinging phosphorous grenades into the truck beds packed with wounded men. After killing several enemy soldiers, Nick was completely out of ammunition. He dropped the rifle and began sprinting toward a narrow-gauge railroad track that ran along the edge of the village. West of the track lay a rice paddy that abutted a small pine forest along the bank of the frozen reservoir. If he could make it to the ice, he could follow the shoreline to the Marine base at Hagaru-ri.

With only an occasional PLA rifle shot groping blindly for him in the darkness, Nick climbed in a culvert under the rail track and slid across a frozen stream to the rice paddy. Staying low, he ran across the paddy to a snow-covered stack of rice stalks in the middle of the field. First, Nick heard the eerie Chinese whistles in the distance, then he saw the bright-red splotches in the moonlit snow. Throwing himself behind the stack of rice stalks, he came face-to-face with an RCT-31 rifleman whose left leg was wrapped in a bloody T-shirt. Nick wasted no time. "Gotta get into the forest. Give me your arm."

The wounded man, with his arm wrapped around Nick's neck, was able to bear weight on his right leg, but could only advance with a strenuous, one-legged hop. Nick didn't know what to do. Carry him on his back? That would be suicide. But they sure as hell weren't going anywhere fast this way.

"Need some help?" A broad-shouldered, young Corporal stepped up and draped the man's other arm over his shoulder. With the wounded man pushing off on his good leg every third stride, they swung along the paddy until they reached the edge of the forest that lined the reservoir.

The wounded man was standing on his good leg, leaning against the trunk of a white pine tree when a single shot rang out. With his eyes widened in surprise, he wavered, then slid down the tree trunk, crumpling slowly like the bellows of a punctured accordion.

"Sniper!" Nick yelled and threw himself to the ground. But the Corporal didn't react fast enough and the sniper's second shot struck him straight in the forehead. Nick rose and ran into the forest.

With whistles and shouts, a company of PLA riflemen clambered down the bank of the railroad track and raced across the rice paddy, firing their weapons at dozens of men of RCT-31 running into the forest. Dodging branches laden with snow, Nick lifted his boots high and churned through the drifts beneath the pines. Clambering across a field of icy boulders, he ran out on the frozen reservoir. 300 feet off the shoreline, he joined a group of RCT-31 survivors heading south. Although most of the men were able-bodied, a few wounded lagged behind the column.

Nick trudged south, periodically glancing back at the shoreline. Strange. There was no more enemy fire. The PLA pursuing them had stopped at the edge of the reservoir. Did the Chinese consider fleeing enemy soldiers no longer fair game? No. Nick watched helplessly as a single, white-quilted soldier, still energized by the chase, ran out on the ice and bayoneted the last American straggler. But now the gunfire had stopped and all was silent except the wailing of the Arctic wind.

Chapter Twenty Nine
Advance in Another Direction

TOKYO—*in the frozen northeast, troops of the United States Seventh Division cut their way back down the eastern shore of the Changjin Reservoir from Sinhung to Hagaru, at the lake's southern extremity. There they made a junction with troops of the First Marine Division, holding the town against a continued enemy attack...Three Chinese regiments, it was estimated, were south of them, blocking the winding road through the mountains that is the sole communications line for the isolated troops to bases on the east coast.*

New York Times
December 3, 1950

Hagaru-ri, DPRK
December 5, 1950

At 0700, after the first good night's sleep in many days, Nick sat on an empty ammunition crate eating a breakfast of canned peaches, ham and pancakes. With the temperature outside at -5°F, the Coleman heaters in the Marine's mess tent were barely able to break freezing. Balancing a mess tray on his knees, Nick broke up a thin layer of ice crystals forming on top of the maple syrup. Then stabbed a pancake with his fork and swabbed it in the cold, slushy syrup. *Man. So delicious. When was the last time he'd had a real breakfast?*

Nick knew he was just lucky to be alive. The last couple of weeks had been disastrous. Only 1000 of the 3200 men in RCT 31 made it safely to the Marine lines at Hagaru-ri. And of those, less than half were still able-bodied.

Nick's new 4th platoon, composed of survivors of RCT-31, was incorporated into the 10,000 man 1st Marine Division at the southern tip of the reservoir. No longer US Army RCT 31, they became the 31st Battalion/7th Marine Regiment/1st Marine Division (*31/7*).

Strange how things had worked out. No *doggie vs. jarhead* taunts here. Nick would never forget how the Marines came out on the ice to sweep the survivors of RCT-31 into their well-fortified position. Now, as part of the 7th Marine Regiment, Nick was beginning to see how the leadership and solid planning of Marine Major General Smith had paid off. Unlike the X Corps commander GEN Almond, who was constantly pushing for a double-time advance to the Yalu, MG Smith had taken time to prepare well. After establishing strongly fortified bases along the Main Supply Route (MSR) at Koto-ri and Hagaru-ri, MG Smith positioned supply depots along the planned northern route of attack from Yudam-ni to the Yalu River. Now, under siege by a large PLA force at Yudam-ni, the Marines, with close air support, were able to complete a 18 mile fighting retreat down the MSR to the main base at Hagaru-ri.

Although the men of his platoon were all Army infantrymen, Nick's new company commander was a Marine Corps Captain. Unlike army recruits, the Marines were an all-volunteer attack force of specialized warriors. Taking the lead in most new operations, they knew the risks were high. So, mistakes were not an option for the Marines.

Sipping his coffee, Nick watched the airfield come alive at dawn. Ground crews, technicians and medical teams swarmed across the landing strip like worker bees rising with the sun. Engines rumbled as trucks and heavy equipment warmed up. Empty stretchers lined the runway awaiting the first rays of dawn. Soon the C 47's would be coming in. Although escorted by B-26 Invaders, the lumbering *gooney birds* were often hit by enemy fire when they came in to land. Yesterday a C-47, struck by enemy fire, had crash landed short of the field.

Bulldozing and blasting around the clock for the past two weeks, the Marine Corps engineers had leveled an air strip large enough for the C-47s to land and take off. At night, while working under floodlights, engineers often had to lay down their tools and take up arms to defend the field from probing attacks by the Chinese. Nick recalled the maxim drilled into new Marine recruits. *Every Marine is first and foremost a rifleman.*

Nick's coffee cup rattled on the mess tray, teetering like a drunk in a sudden, strong wind. Then an olive-green fuselage flashed by the tent window as a C-47 transport thumped down upon the airstrip behind the mess hall. Nick walked out by the C-47 as its prop was spinning down. The ground crew swung open the large cargo door, installed a ramp and began unloading supplies and ammunition. Then, after a company of replacement Marines deplaned, medics began to load the seriously wounded and frostbitten into the cavernous hold of the aircraft. A few of the heavily bandaged men were able to shuffle on board without assistance. But most were wrapped like mummies in down feather casualty bags and carried onto the plane on stretchers.

Deep sorrow surged upward from Nick's chest into his throat as he watched the brisk unloading and loading of cargo shift dramatically into a solemn ritual. With Marines standing at attention on either side of the ramp, the Air Force medics gently layered 30 olive drab body bags, like precious cargo, into the hold. Nick knew the Marines never left their dead behind. A lot more body bags would be loaded onto flights going out today.

Kaleidoscopic images swept across Nick's mind. *Orange-red bursts above his head. Earth and rocks soaring through the air. The buzz of swarming shrapnel. Curses and screams. Bullets whizzing by. The thud as a man reels backwards. The savage thrust of a bayonet into flesh. Blood on snow. Brave men falling beside him.*

A distant hum increasing to an engine roar snapped Nick's attention back to the present. Then a thump and the squeak of tires as a B 26 Invader touched down on the runway. With a brisk shake of his head, Nick cleared his mind and walked across the field to the flight operations Quonset hut.

When he received the message that Ramón would be refueling between flights, Nick felt a rush of anticipation. So much had happened since they last met in Busan. At times he felt he wouldn't survive the retreat from the Chosin Reservoir. It would be great to restore some sense of normalcy in all this madness.

Soon Ramón strode out of flight ops onto the edge of the runway with his helmet in his hand. In a dark blue cold-weather parka, flight pants and rubberized boots, Nick thought Ramón looked like one of the spacemen in the film Destination Moon.

"Hey, buddy!" Ramón said with a firm handshake and one hand grasping Nick's forearm. "I was afraid you were done for."

Nick laughed. "That goes double for me! We did have some close calls. What's up for you now?"

"Got to be back in the air right away. A couple of more runs today. Just wanted to be sure you were OK."

"Thanks man. It looks like you fly boys really helped the Marines coming down from Yudam-ni. Scuttlebutt now is you'll be flying some nighttime ops as well."

"Yeah. With the new night radar we can do some damage. You heading south soon?"

"We'll be on the MSR tomorrow."

"Don't worry. I'll have your back all the way down to the coast."

Ramón's copilot beckoned from the door of flight ops. "Got to get going, pal. Be seeing you!"

After his brief, but invigorating encounter with Ramón, Nick trudged back on the grimy path of compacted snow to the men of his new platoon. The rest of the day would be spent preparing for tomorrow's 60 mile breakout down the MSR to the port of Hungnam. Nick's major concern was keeping his platoon's weapons operational in the extreme cold weather. Rifles and automatic weapons were working at half capacity. The timing of hand grenades was uncertain. Unstable mortar propellant could rain short rounds on the Marine fox holes. Frozen shell powder charges reduced the accuracy of artillery fire. Careful cleaning, warming and occasional discharge of weapons was required throughout the day.

With his righthand man SGT Mike Miller now dead, and only a few of his old team still combat ready, Nick had to cobble together a new rifle team. Fortunately, SGT Frank Riley, re-assigned to Nick's 4th platoon from another decimated RCT-31 unit, was a seasoned combat veteran.

Sitting close to the space heater in the tent he shared with Nick, SGT Riley was cleaning excess lubrication from the barrel of his M1 to keep it from freezing. "What's up, Lieutenant? We pulling out tomorrow?"

Nick pulled off his gloves and rubbed his hands together inches above the heater. "We're pushing off at daybreak, Frank. But get this. General Smith says it won't be a retreat. We're just going to advance in a different direction."

Riley laughed. "I like that. The old man's got balls."

At 1700 Nick and SGT Riley walked along the perimeter of 31/7. Dug in deep behind rows of barbed wire and a barricade of sandbags and logs, the 4th platoon held a strong position between the crossfire of automatic rifle and machine gun crews. But he was worried. New intel estimated that several full divisions of the PLA were gathering in the hills surrounding Hagaru-ri. Up to now, the PLA had mounted only small probes to assess the Marine defenses. But a full-scale attack to prevent a break out was likely at any moment. Nick looked across the open field east of the Marine base. Winter twilight seemed to layer the snow with the violet-blue cloak of death.

At 2200 a muffled boom, like the sound of a distant kettle drum, was followed by three, shrill whistle blasts. Then a flare burst overhead illuminating the field with brilliant, white phosphorus light. With an eerie cacophony of bugles, cymbals, whistles and drums, a horde of screaming Chinese soldiers, charged out of the darkness surrounding the Marine's line of defense. *Kill! Kill! Marines!*

Running, falling and leaping up again, white quilted Chinese soldiers fired burp guns and tossed stick grenades as they charged directly into the field of automatic weapons and machine gun fire. Most of the PLA fell, but some made it through.

Nick had been here before—just as he anticipated, squads of PLA began to probe the line, searching for vulnerable seams to break through. Well disciplined by SGT Riley, Nick's riflemen held their fire until the Chinese were only 25 yards away. Wave after wave of PLA charged the line, fell, staggered to their feet and charged again. When most of the attackers had fallen, new PLA soon took their place.

At 2400 four B-26 Invaders from Yonpo airfield near Hungnam arrived to strafe and bomb the attacking Chinese forces. Recently equipped with more accurate radar than previously available, the B 26s were able to drop bombs within 1000 yards of the front line. Although PLA attacks paused after a bombing run, they soon resumed, continuing throughout the night. Firing and reloading his M1 as fast as he could at the charging PLA, Nick wondered if Ramón was up there helping out.

The few enemy soldiers who penetrated the perimeter were soon killed in savage hand-to-hand fighting. At 0400, when Marine howitzers and mortars finally found the proper range of enemy artillery and mortar batteries, the PLA attacks began to falter.

At dawn ice crystals in the air glinted in the sunlight over the silent battlefield. Hundreds of dead Chinese soldiers lay like twisted rag dolls in the cratered field beside the airstrip, their bloody, white uniforms dusted with snow. Nick and SGT Riley surveyed their position. Two dead PLA lay in frozen patches of blood just inside the perimeter. Three men in Nick's platoon had been killed and six wounded. Although he scarcely knew any of his new men, Nick was proud of their performance. This was a team he could count on during the upcoming break out.

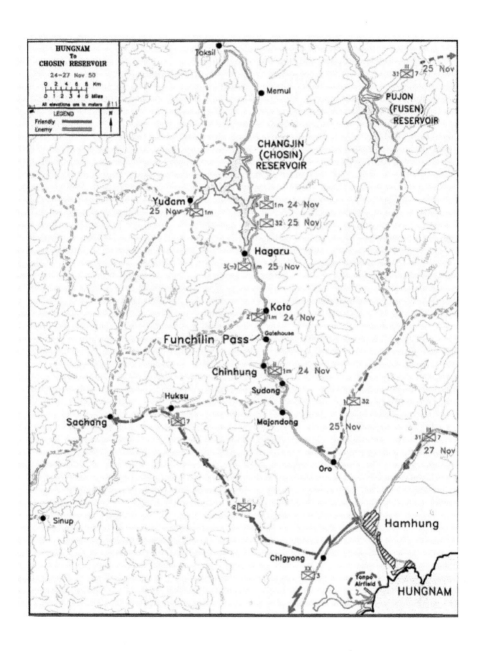

Chapter Thirty
Breakout

CROSSROADS IN KOREA—*The Eighth Army, outflanked and outnumbered, retreated toward the 38th parallel, while the Tenth Corps, overextended and dispersed in the 7,000-foot mountains and thirty below cold of Northern Korea, fought bitterly to escape destruction...*

New York Times
December 6, 1950

MSR to the Port of Hungnam
December 6, 1950

At 0600 the night air was thick with smoke from burning supplies and detonated equipment not to be left behind for the enemy. Charged with clearing the high ground above the MSR in advance of the convoy, Nick's 4th platoon marched south behind tanks of the 7th Marine Regiment toward their next fortified position at Koto-ri. Leapfrogging each other down the road, one half of the Marine artillery battalion maintained continuous fire on enemy positions as the other half moved south.

At 0730 two gull-winged, Navy Corsairs breaking through the heavy morning clouds, came in low with their engines whistling death. The first plane dropped a tank of napalm on a PLA rifle team and machine gun nest above the road. The second plane flew through the thick, acrid smoke to rake the burning terrain with its 20 mm cannons and rockets. Nick's platoon then advanced to root out any PLA still dug in after the aerial attack.

An odor like gasoline mixed with laundry detergent wafted through the smoky black air as Nick approached the target area. Flaming napalm clung like burning rubber to the blackened bodies of three PLA clustered around their smoldering machine gun nest. Nearby, charred bodies of riflemen lay steaming in the snow.

As Nick's point man approached the PLA position, a sudden burp gun blast cut him down. "Where?" Nick yelled.

"Behind those boulders," SGT Riley shouted as he pulled the pin on his grenade and lobbed it 50 feet in the air. With a fusillade of M1 fire, Nick's men rushed in and killed the PLA survivors.

Chaotic fighting soon slowed the convoy's headway to several miles per hour. At almost every turn, there was a PLA roadblock of rocks, timber and sandbags with machine guns dug in on both sides of the road. Following a Sherman tank toward a roadblock, half of Nick's men ran in a skirmish line low to the ground, then dropped and rolled over in the snow like Siberian Huskies before continuing their charge. The other half of his platoon did the same thing, overlapping the first group. When the PLA position was overrun, a half-track cleared the road of debris.

Nick was startled as they passed several dead PLA lying beside two dead Marines. *Are we really so different?* Wearing US parkas and boots, the Chinese were difficult to distinguish from the Americans.

The combined efforts of riflemen, artillery, heavy weapons, tanks, B-26s and Corsairs were able to clear the PLA from the road and high ground in front of the convoy. But as soon as the Marine lead force moved south, fresh PLA troops scrambled up the slopes like long-tailed *goral* mountain goats to continue the attack. The 5th Marines bringing up the rear of the convoy would have to deal with fire from the high ground all over again. As the convoy inched further south, the Chinese became more daring. PLA snipers began targeting truck drivers while a few bold infantrymen raced along the side of the road hurling hand grenades and gasoline bombs into the truck beds.

All afternoon Air Force and Navy aircraft napalmed and strafed the MSR as Nick's platoon cleared PLA from roadblocks and the high ground. Losses were heavy on both sides. By dusk, enemy attacks on the convoy seemed smaller, less fierce. With such losses, Nick wondered how long the PLA could keep it up. *Maybe they were running out of gas?*

Koto-ri DPRK

December 7, 1950

Bone tired and freezing, Nick's platoon trudged into the heavily fortified Marine base at Koto-ri shortly after dark. The temperature had already fallen below zero. Passing through the guard post, Nick felt he was entering a safe cocoon—if only for a night. Truck engines hummed in the motor pool. Dim light radiating from within their canvas walls turned tents into golden pyramids spread across the snow covered field. The PLA was not likely to come tonight. They wouldn't waste their dwindling resources on an attack against a strong Marine position. They'd wait for the breakout to continue south tomorrow.

As they approached the sandbagged Marine headquarters, the platoon came to an abrupt halt. Men in olive green parkas were unloading dead Marines from an idling three-quarter ton truck. Temporarily stacked in the snow by the roadside, the frozen dead were bathed in frosty, silver moonlight. Nick released an icy breath. Did two of his men lie there? That's what it cost today.

In a staff meeting with the battalion commander, Nick learned that total Marine casualties for the 38-hour withdrawal from Hagaru-ri were 103 dead, 493 wounded and 7 missing.

"How many casualties in your platoon, Lieutenant?" The battalion commander asked.

"Two dead. Three wounded. One missing, sir."

"So you're in pretty good shape. Dismissed."

On the way to the tent he shared with SGT Riley a light snowfall layered Nick's eyebrows with icy crystals. *In pretty good shape? Jesus.* Isn't that what McLean said to Almond just before the shit hit the fan at the reservoir? He was down six men and they were only midway down the MSR. Up next was the Funchilin Pass where the PLA were surely entrenched.

Inside the tent SGT Riley sat wrapped in a sleeping bag beside the space heater. "Man, these jarheads sure run a choice hotel, Lieutenant." He pointed to a small bottle of gasoline next to a coffee can half filled with dirt. "Even got us a little cooking stove."

"Pretty classy all right. But I'm still freezing my ass off." Nick unlaced his leather shoepacs, removed the icy, felt insoles and pulled off two pair of wool socks. "Damn insoles froze up again with sweat." He sat down by the heater and began rubbing his pale blue toes. "Lucky there's no frostbite."

"Not yet, Lieutenant. Still got a ways to go." SGT Riley held up a can of C rations. "How about cheese hamburgers and gravy tonight? The fire'll scorch the beef and the gravy might just melt the frozen insides."

The camp was quiet when, layered with every possible piece of clothing, Nick and SGT Riley lay head to toe inside their sleeping bags. SGT Riley immediately plunged into the dark sleep of exhaustion. Nick was able to grasp several moments of reverie before falling asleep.

The soft down pillow. The brush of Ruth's hair across his cheek. Her body folded against his back.

Funchilin Pass
December 9, 1950

The grade rose steeply around each curve as Nick's platoon trudged up the snow covered road toward the top of the pass. With the weariness in his legs counterbalanced by hyper alert muscles in his chest and arms, Nick remained ready for battle at every turn. The white uniforms of the PLA were almost invisible in the snow. But they *had* to be dug in somewhere near the top.

Then the point man raised an arm and everyone dropped to a knee. Nick ran low to the point and scanned the summit. *What the hell?* He thought he'd seen everything but this was over the edge. PLA machine gunners and riflemen manning

295

the roadblock were layered with ice and snow—frozen like icicle soldiers in their defensive positions. Some were heavily blanketed in white while others had been sculpted by the wind into phantom fighting positions. A rifleman lay prone, carefully sighting his weapon. An assistant gunner fed his machine gun a belt of ammunition covered with icicles.

Nick was stunned. *Frozen in good fighting position.* What courage and discipline. PLA casualties were much higher than ours. Was this all worth it? How many more men will die on both sides until we get the hell out of here?

Nick's platoon proceeded downhill until they were forced to halt before a treadway bridge that had twice been blown up by the PLA and repaired each time by US Army and Marine engineers. Now, once again detonated by the enemy, the engineers were preparing to reconstruct the bridge with supplies air dropped from C-119 flying boxcars. Nick watched as the twin-tailed C-119s rumbled in low, drawing small arms fire from the PLA, as they dropped 2500 pound steel bridge sections attached to huge parachutes. Within a few hours the bridge was once again open to heavy vehicular traffic.

Nick released the tension in his body. Now all that stood between his men and the downhill slope was an army of winter ghosts scattered across the high ground without any fortifications on the road. Soon they met Marine reinforcements coming up the MSR from the south. Brushing past a column of Marines with shoulder thumps and warm banter, Nick felt strangely light footed. The PLA had lost a lot of men and their attacks were losing strength. Maybe now his platoon could cruise all the way to the seaport of Hungnam.

The Chinese mounted repeated attacks along the route but were repulsed each time. Ten miles south of Koto-ri, the PLA managed to swarm onto the road at Sudong-ni. But a counterattack by the 1st Marines soon drove them off into the hills. There were no more significant Chinese attacks along the road to the Port of Hungnam.

Port of Hungnam

Christmas Eve 1950

The 1st Marine Division's total losses for the withdrawal from Hagaru-ri were 178 dead, 749 wounded, and 23 missing. Additionally, there were 1,534 non-battle casualties, mostly frostbite. Chinese losses were unreported, but appeared to be very much higher.

When the convoy arrived at the Hungnam perimeter which was manned by US Army and Marine forces, Nick's platoon was folded back into the Army's 7th Division like lost sheep. Nick had mixed feelings. Hands-down, GEN Smith was a better leader than GEN Almond; and the Marines were an elite, well disciplined force. Nevertheless, he felt comfortable being back with the Army guarding the perimeter from possible enemy attack while 193 Navy and Merchant Marine ships in the harbor prepared for evacuation.

The Marines were up first on the boarding list. *Fair enough* Nick thought. The Marines fought long and hard. *And they probably saved my ass.* They've earned the heroic credits. Next up were the men of 1/32 IN. They'd lived through hell up on the reservoir. Left alone on the east side under attack by overwhelming forces, the survivors fought well and hard.

Although never really a leatherneck, Nick was back in the Army again.

Nick's battle weary platoon marched past a cordon of military police and knifed its way through a huge crowd of Korean refugees thronging the harbor. Although they had planned to evacuate government officials and their families, the UN command had not anticipated this flood of refugees trying to escape the advancing Chinese forces.

Like guardian angels, the crews of the transport ships stepped up and evacuated more than 80,000 civilians from the port. Most were packed in holds or crowded onto cargo decks. A few were flown out of nearby Yonpo airfield.

Within a ring of fire from two cruisers, six destroyers, three medium landing ships, the battleship Missouri and a squadron of B-26 attack bombers, Nick's Merchant Marine transport ship steamed out of the harbor on Christmas Eve. Sitting on a bunk deep in the bowels of the SS *Norfolk Victory*, Nick uncorked a small flask of Jack Daniels he'd been carrying in his field jacket for just this occasion. "Merry Christmas, Frank," he said taking a swig and passing the flask to SGT Riley. "Damn good work."

Kaboom! A thunderous explosion rocked the ship as an enormous cloud of smoke and dust swirled the twisted rubble of piers, cranes, warehouses and heavy equipment high above the port of Hungnam.

SGT Riley raised the flask. "And here's to the frogman demolition team."

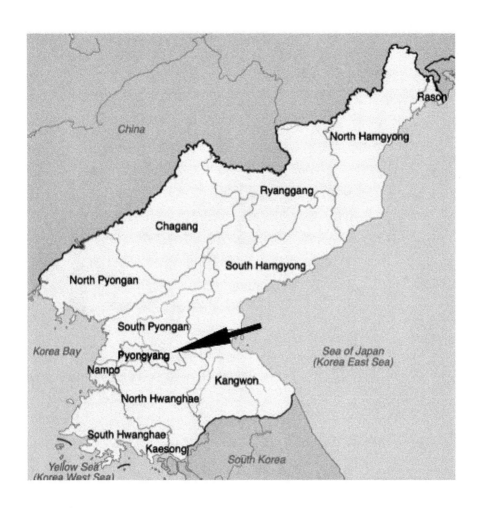

China

Rason

North Hamgyong

Ryanggang

Chagang

South Hamgyong

North Pyongan

South Pyongan

Korea Bay

Pyongyang

Sea of Japan
(Korea East Sea)

Nampo

Kangwon

North Hwanghae

South Hwanghae

Kaesong

South Korea

Yellow Sea
(Korea West Sea)

Chapter Thirty One
Twilight in Pyongyang

PYONGYANG—*The heroic Peoples Army and guerrillas, in close cooperation with the brotherly Chinese Peoples Volunteers, have already liberated almost all the areas north of the 38th parallel, including Pyongyang...and are now continuing a large scale annihilation program in pursuit of the enemy who are fleeing southward in confusion.*

> Kim Il-sung, Supreme Commander NKPA
> Celebration of the liberation of Pyongyang
> December 9, 1950

Pyongyang DPRK
December 9, 1950

In a light snowfall, Ho-jun and Min-ji climbed the weathered, granite steps leading up to his parents' house in the Moranbong District. While she was dressed in traditional high-waisted Hanbok style for the victory celebration, Ho-jun wore his NKPA dress uniform at his father's request. With a broad smile, the housemaid Nari opened the main gate and ushered them through the inner courtyard. As he mounted the steps to the main house, Ho-jun trailed his fingertips across the snow covered branches of a plum tree. The icy sensation

301

triggered sweet melancholia. How often had he and his childhood friend Kwang-min staged snowball fights in this court yard?

Removing their shoes at the vestibule, Ho-jun and Min-ji donned slippers and followed Nari into the main hall where Ho-jun's father, mother and younger sister Jung-soon, all dressed in Hanbok style, rose to meet them. Ho-jun and Min-ji greeted his parents with deep, respectful bows. Then they exchanged lesser bows with Jung-soon.

Unexpectedly, Ho-jun's father stepped forward and laid a hand on his son's shoulder. "Your service to our country will not be forgotten, Ho-jun. I am proud of you."

Bathed in soft winter light filtering through the leaded glass windows, Ho-jun bowed deeply. A warm sensation flowed into his cheeks, then spread downward into his chest with an overwhelming sense of sorrow. He had seen so much carnage in the past six months. He felt more like a survivor than a hero. "Thank you father. I am honored."

Min-ji caught his eye with a subtle tilt of her head. *Are you all right, yeobo?* She silently asked. Ho-jun nodded. How lucky he felt to have such a wife.

In the dining area Nari had laid out a festive dinner of diced cabbage *kimchi*, marinated chicken *dakgalbi* and *congee* rice porridge. Everyone except his father sat on mats around the table. He preferred the old custom of sitting directly on the heated floor because he believed it led to a calm and peaceful state of mind.

Nari placed a pitcher of cold *soju* rice wine on the table and stepped back. Ho-jun's father filled everyone's glass, including one for Nari, and proposed a toast. "For the sake of our country. *Geonbae!"*

Ho-jun raised his glass. "And for our family."

Everyone took a sip of soju from their small ceramic cups.

Still astonished by the sudden turn in the war, Ho-jun glanced around the table with warm satisfaction. Everyone seemed to be doing well. Min-ji was stimulated by her curriculum development work for the Pyongyang public school system. Using natural forms and bold colors, his mother was producing fine calligraphy. His father's medical practice was thriving and his sister was enjoying her work as an assistant to the dean of the medical school.

Ho-jun leaned back and sipped his soju. This was uncanny. Just a few weeks ago he was running for his life. Now the UN forces had retreated all the way to Seoul. The Americans were probably very tired of fighting in Korea. *Could we be nearing the end of this war?*

After dinner Jung-soon brought out her *kayakeum* zither and sat cross legged on the floor. Sliding the moveable bridges up and down, she plucked the twelve strings with her thumb and fingers to produce the melody that meant so much to *all* Koreans North and South—*Arirang*.

When the Japanese colonial government made it a criminal offense to sing any patriotic Korean song, Arirang became the unofficial anthem. Everyone joined in to sing the heartfelt lyrics.

My love, you are leaving me
Your feet will be sore before you go ten ri.

Just as there are many stars in the clear sky,
There are also many dreams in our heart.
There, over there is Baekdu Mountain,
Where, even in the middle of winter days, flowers bloom.

Pyongyang, DPRK
January 3, 1951

At 1000 the sky was clear with a temperature of -1°C when Ho-jun came out of a Medical Corps staff meeting in the Ministry of Defense building. Crossing Kim Il-sung Square, he walked on a path packed with crusty snow toward the provisional NKPA field hospital that was temporarily located in an abandoned warehouse on the bank of the Taedong River. He was in no hurry. Directing a team of two junior physicians, SGT Hak, six medics and a nursing staff, he had scheduled medical rounds for 1100. Most of the patients had problems quite familiar to Ho-jun—battlefield wounds and injuries, amputations, burns, dysentery, pneumonia and the perennial wintertime enemy frostbite.

Although the war was still raging, Ho-jun was feeling reasonably content. Pyongyang had remained quiet since the American bombing of the airfield a few weeks ago. He was back in his apartment next to Kimmy Boi Park with Min-ji. And the enemy was on the run! Soon, the Americans would have to evacuate Seoul. Victory appeared at hand.

Passing the snow covered Taedong Gate, Ho-jun peered through the steamy window of a storefront shop at a young woman who was deep frying *tteokbakki*. He looked at his watch. Why not? The field hospital was only a few blocks away. He had enough time for a couple of these delicious rice cakes.

Ho-jun sat on a frosty wooden bench by the river and removed a glove. Watching a barge cruise slowly down the Taedong, he dipped his fish rice cake into the sweet red chili sauce. *Delicious.* He could skip lunch at the hospital canteen today.

Rrrrummmm. A low pitched, humming sound drew his attention to the western sky. *Mapsosa!* A formation of B-29 bombers was approaching the city. Running for cover beneath the curved roof of an ancient pavilion, Ho-jun thought he heard a flock of startled pigeons fly up. But there were no pigeons in the sky—only bundles of incendiary sticks breaking apart then streaming down on the city with a sound like a waterfall.

A bamboo fence beside the pavilion burst into flame. Like bellows, the alleys between the half-timbered buildings expelled a scorching wind across the ground that fanned the flames. The sky glowed red and flames leapt like flashes of lightning at sunset.

As black smoke billowed across the street, Ho-jun pulled his scarf up to cover his face and began picking his way through the rubble and flames. Then came a second wave of bombers. Just before the demolition bombs hit, Ho-jun heard a whirring sound, then a thud that shook the earth beneath his feet. Doors flew off houses, windows blew out and entire buildings clattered to the ground.

Ho-jun's heart pounded against his chest. His nostrils were clogged with sticky particles of soot and his eyes stung with acrid tears. With red and yellow flames prancing through the streets like drunken *dokkaebi* demons, he was uncertain in which direction he should go. Looking north he could see there was almost total destruction—the field hospital was probably gone.

His mind was racing. Was Min-ji safe at school in the northern part of the city? Had his parent's neighborhood been bombed? What about Jung-soon at the medical school office? The entire city was in flames. Where could he go to find more information about his family and join the medical rescue team? Maybe the University Hospital had escaped a direct hit. Dodging fallen debris and scattered bodies, Ho-jun sprinted through the surging flames like an ancient *Gojoseon* war horse.

Epilogue

From 1950-1953, combined incendiary and demolition bombing destroyed 75 percent of the buildings in Pyongyang. At the end of the war an estimated 50,000 people of its prewar population of 500,000 remained in the city.

The Korean War continued back and forth around the 38th parallel for two more years. Total UN military dead and missing were 162,394 South Koreans, 36,574 Americans and 4,544 other UN forces. Total Communist military losses were 335,000–526,000 North Koreans, 208,729–400,000 Chinese and 299 Russians.

Nearly 3 million people died in the Korean War—more than half were civilians. Total estimated civilian deaths in the war were 990,968 South Koreans and 1,500,000 North Koreans.

Wikipedia.org/wiki/Korean_War

Author's Note

Like many American boys, I played war games as a child in the 1950s. I even had my grandfather make me a toy machine gun from an old roll of masking tape and a broomstick handle. As an adult, I have always liked high quality war movies. But I never considered myself a war buff until I retired from a stimulating career in academic medicine and moved to the Oregon coast. It was here that I learned of a 1942 Japanese submarine attack on an army fort at the mouth of the Columbia River. Further research revealed that the same submarine had returned to firebomb the Oregon forest. And just before the end of the war, a Japanese balloon bomb lodged in a tree was responsible for the death of a minister's wife and a group of teenagers on a church picnic.

Fascinated to learn of these attacks on US soil about the time I was born, I decided to research the issue and write about the events with fictionalized characters—but paying particular attention to historical facts. Following extensive research, consultation with military veterans and historians and several trips to Japan, I published the historical fiction novel Enemy in the Mirror: Love and Fury in the Pacific War (Amazon). With American and Japanese protagonists, I attempted to portray both sides in the conflict.

After comprehensive research, consultation and trips to Europe, Mexico and the East Coast USA, I published my second novel The Osprey and Sea Wolf: The Battle of the Atlantic 1942 (Amazon). In that book, my protagonists were a Mexican American Air Force pilot and a German U-boat captain.

Somewhere along the line, I realized that my major interest was in understanding America and her enemies in the wars that have occurred during my lifetime. My website www.enemyinmirror.com is intended to promote understanding of America and her enemies in wartime.

In this historical fiction novel, I follow the chain of events from 1940 to 1950 through the imagined lives of two young men: A North Korean physician, caught up in the wars against Imperial Japan and America; and an American infantry officer who is a veteran of the bloody New Guinea campaign against Imperial Japan. Ironically, two men who fought a common enemy in the Pacific War have now become enemies.

Acknowledgments

Hoffman Center Critique Group
Kay Stolz, and Marcia Silver

Consultants
Kim Davenport - Tacoma Historical Society; Archangelo DiFante - US Air Force Historical Research Agency; William McLaughlin - US Air Force National Museum; Lindsay Muha - National Archives and Records Administration; Valentin Pak - President, Vladivostok Korean-Russian community; Karl Lewis Polifka - COL USAF (Ret.); Professor Igor Tolstokulakov, School of Regional and International Studies Far Eastern Federal University, Vladivostok; Lee Walker - LTC USN (Ret.); Charles Thornsvard - COL US Army (Ret.).

Manuscript Reviewers
Angela Angelini, Gary Antonides, Will Austin, Bob Balmer, Betsy Buddy, Lauren Cobb, Steve Evans, Doug Fenton, Pamela Helms, Daisha Kissel, Bob LeRoy, Jerry McGee, Sherry Scull, and Jann Smith

Online Resources
PBS American Experience: The Battle of Chosin; History.com; Korean War Everything/Facebook; Korean War Pics and Stories/Facebook; Korean War Project/Facebook; The Korean War's Chosin Reservoir/Facebook; Quora; Truman Library; US Air Force Historical Research Agency; US Army Center of Military History; US Marine Corps History Division; Wikipedia; Wilson Center

I wish to express particular gratitude for two individuals who have consulted with me throughout the long process of writing this book:

Oleg Pak, MD, PhD
Medical Center Director
Far Eastern Federal University
Vladivostok Russia

Jwa-Seop Shin, MD, PhD
Chair, Department of Medical Education
Seoul National University College of Medicine
Seoul Korea

Finally, I want to thank my wife Holly Evans Smith who has travelled throughout the world with me on this project and reviewed the manuscript at every stage of its development.

Selected Bibliography

Alexander, Bevin. *Korea. The First War We Lost.* New York: Hippocrene Books 1986.

Appleman, Roy E. *East of Chosin. Entrapment and Breakout in Korea 1950.* College Station: Texas A&M University Press 1987.

Armstrong, Charles K. *The North Korean Revolution 1945-1950.* Ithaca: Cornell University Press 2003.

Blair, Clay. *The Forgotten War. America in Korea 1950-1953.* New York: Doubleday 1988.

Brady, James. *The Coldest War. A Memoir of Korea.* New York: St. Martin's Press 1990.

Cummings, Bruce. *The Korean War. A History.* New York: Random House 2010.

Fehrenbach, T.R. *This kind of War, The Classic Korean War History.* New York: Macmillan 1963.

George, Alexander. *The Chinese Communist Army in Action. The Korean War and its Aftermath.* New York: Columbia University Press 1967.

Halberstram, David. *The Coldest Winter. America and the Korean War.* New York: Hyperion 2007.

Hastings, Max. *The Korean War.* New York: Simon and Schuster 1987.

Kang, Hildi. *Under the Black Umbrella. Voices from Colonial Korea 1910-1945.* Ithaca: Cornell University Press 2001.

Lankov, Andrei. *The Real North Korea. Life and Politics in the Failed Stalinist Utopia.* New York: Oxford University Press 2015.

Li, Xiaobing. *Attack at Chosin. The Chinese Second Offensive in Korea*. Norman: The University of Oklahoma Press 2020.

Myers, B.R. *The Cleanest Race. How North Koreans See Themselves*. New York: Melville House 2010.

Minnich, James M. *The North Korean People's Army. Origins and Current Tactics*. Annapolis: Naval Institute Press 2005.

Oberdorfer, Don. *The Two Koreas. A Contemporary History*. New York: Penguin 1997.

Russ, Martin. *Breakout. The Chosin Reservoir Campaign Korea 1950*. New York: Penguin Books 1999.

Su, Dae-sook. *Kim Il-sung. The North Korean Leader*. New York: Columbia University Press 1988.

Toland, John. *In Mortal Combat. Korea 1950-1953*. New York: William Morrow 1991.

Tomedi, Rudy. *No Bugles, No Drums. An Oral History of the Korean War*. New York: John Wiley 1993.

Wilson, Jim. *Retreat, Hell! The Epic Story of the 1st Marines in Korea*. New York: William Morrow 1988.

Yom, Sang-stop. *Three Generations* (English translation). Brooklyn: Archipelago Books 2005.

ARMY	
Corps	2+ Divisions
Division	3+ Brigades
Brigade or Regiment	3-5 Battalions
Battalion	3-5 Companies
Company	3-4 Platoons
Platoon	3-4 Squads
Squad	6-10 Soldiers

United States Army Organization

GLOSSARY

1/32 IN - US Army 1st Battalion/32 Infantry Regiment

88th Special Rifle Brigade - Soviet international military unit

Arisaka 97 - standard Imperial Japanese Army sniper rifle

Atabrine - Trade name for antimalarial drug quinacrine

Bazooka - shoulder-type rocket launcher

B-25 - North American medium bomber

B-26 - Martin medium bomber

BAR - Browning automatic rifle

CI&E - Allied Command Civil Information and Education

Chosin Reservoir - Japanese name for Changjin Reservoir

Corsair - Vought F-4U carrier-based aircraft

C-119 - Fairchild flying boxcar transport aircraft

C-47 - Douglas Skytrain military transport aircraft

Dai Ichi building - MacArthur's HQ in Tokyo

DPRK - Democratic People's Republic of (North) Korea

Gando Special Force - Manchukuo Imperial Army battalion

GAZ-67 - four-wheel drive Soviet military vehicle

Gojoseon Kingdom - first Korean kingdom until 108 BCE

Goryeo Kingdom - Korean dynasty founded in 918

G2 - US Army Division level intelligence staff

Halftrack - US Army vehicle, wheels in front, track in back

Heijō - Imperial Japanese name for Pyongyang

Hwarang Warriors - Silla Kingdom until 10th Century

Ilyushin - Soviet transport airplane

Inminban - Neighborhood Watch Committee, North Korea

Ka-Bar - US Marine Corps combat knife

KATUSA - South Korean Army augmentation force

Katyusha - Soviet multiple rocket launcher

Keijo - Imperial Japanese name for Seoul

Kempeitai - Imperial Japanese military and secret police force

Kempo - Japanese martial art

K9 East - Busan Korea Air Base

LCI - amphibious infantry landing craft

LVT - amphibious tracked landing craft

Mitsubishi Zero - Imperial Japanese carrier-based fighter

Mogwai - Chinese demons who seek to harm humans

MSR - Main service route

M4 Sherman - US medium-sized tank

M46 Patton - medium-sized tank replacing M4 Sherman

M1 Carbine - lightweight semi-automatic rifle

M1 Garand - standard US infantry semi-automatic rifle

M18 Grenade - US Army colored, smoke grenade

NAJUA - Northeast Anti-Japanese United Army

Nambu Type 92 - Imperial Japanese heavy machine gun

Napalm - naphthalene and palmitate incendiary substance

NKPA - North Korean People's Army

PLA - Chinese People's Liberation Army

PPSh-41 - Soviet submachine "burp" gun

PVA - Chinese People's Volunteer Army

RCT-31 - 31st Regimental Combat Team/7th Infantry Division

Rodong Sinmun - Workers' Party of Korea newspaper

ROK Army - Republic of (South) Korea Army

SCAP - Supreme Commander of Allied Powers

Seppuku - Japanese ritual suicide Harakiri

Sunset Division - US Army 41st Infantry Division

S2 - US Army unit level security and intelligence staff

S3 - US Army battalion level operations planning staff

T-34 tank - Soviet medium tank

Tokkō - Imperial Japanese "Thought" Police

Trench Mortar - portable mortar used in trench warfare

Type 67 Stick Grenade - Chinese "potato masher"

X Corps - US Army 10th Corps

Yaoguai - Chinese ghost monster

Yangban - highest social class of the Korean Chosŏn dynasty

Yeobo - Korean endearment "honey"

ZIS-5V - Soviet 4x2 cargo truck

ZIS-150 - Soviet cargo truck replacing ZIS-5